English
Olympiad

Highly useful for all school students participating
in Various Olympiads & Competitions

English Olympiad

Highly useful for all school students participating in Various Olympiads & Competitions

Series Editor Keshav Mohan
Author Gajendra Singh

Class 6

arihant

ARIHANT PRAKASHAN, MEERUT

ARIHANT PRAKASHAN, MEERUT

All Rights Reserved

ॐ **Administrative & Production Offices**

Corporate Office 'Ramchhaya' 4577/15, Agarwal Road, Darya Ganj New Delhi -110002
Tele: 011- 47630600, 43518550; Fax: 011- 23280316

Head Office Kalindi, TP Nagar, Meerut (UP) - 250002
Tele: 0121-2401479, 2512970, 4004199; Fax: 0121-2401648

All disputes subject to Meerut (UP) jurisdiction only.

ॐ **Sales & Support Offices**

Agra, Ahmedabad, Bengaluru, Bhubaneswar, Bareilly, Chennai, Delhi, Guwahati, Haldwani, Hyderabad, Jaipur, Jalandhar, Jhansi, Kolkata, Kota, Lucknow, Meerut, Nagpur & Pune

ॐ **ISBN** 978-93-5203-407-9

ॐ **Price** ₹80

Typeset by Arihant DTP Unit at Meerut
Printed & Bound by Arihant Publications (I) Ltd. (Press Unit)

Production Team

Publishing Manager	Mahendra Singh Rawat	*Page Layouting*	Diwakar Gaur
Project Head	Karishma Yadav	*DTP Operator*	Vinay Sharma
Project Coordinator	Divya Gusain	*Cover Designer*	Syed Darin Zaidi
Proof Reader	Megha Tiwari & Chetna Sharma	*Inner Designer*	Deepak Kumar

For further information about the products from Arihant
log on to www.arihantbooks.com or email to info@arihantbooks.com

Preface

English Olympiad Series for Class 6th -10th is a series of books which will challenge the young inquisitive minds by the non-routine and exciting Questions on the use of English.

The main purpose of this series is to make the students ready for competitive exams, as English Language is an integral section of almost all competitive examinations. All the questions given in this series are objective in nature so they will provide students a feel of competitive examinations as school/board exams are of qualifying nature but not competitive, which mainly have objective questions.

- **Need of Olympiad Series**
  This series helps students who are willing to sharpen their proficiency in the field of English language. Unlike typical assessment books, which emphasise on drilling practice, the focus of this series is on practising problem solving techniques. It will help the students use the concepts they have learnt to discover that they can actually solve questions.

- **Development of Communication Skills**
  Application based questions given in this series will help students to attain a deeper understanding of different concepts of English Language through which students will be able to imbibe more effective communication skills in themselves.

- **Complement Your School Studies**
  This series complements the additional preparation needs of students for regular school/board exams. By learning English effectively, students will not only be able to perform well in English language exam but also they will perform better in Science/Social Science/Mathematics where medium to write the answer is English. Along with, it will also address all the requirements of the students who are approaching National/State level competitions or Olympiads.

We shall welcome criticism from the students, teachers, educators and parents. We shall also like to hear from all of you about errors and shortcomings which may have remained in this edition and the suggestions for their improvement in the next edition.

Editor & Author

Contents

Chapter 1

Nouns and Pronouns

Nouns

Nouns are simply the names we give to everything around us, whether it be a person, an event, a place or an object, etc. Every particular name used to define something is a noun for.
e.g. Amsterdam, India, Blackberry, Water, Honesty, etc.

Types of Nouns

Following are the types of nouns

Proper Nouns These are the names given to something to make them more specific. Proper nouns are written with capital letters
e.g. Monday, London, Australia, Atlantic Ocean, Ramesh etc.

Common Nouns These are used for a class of person, place or thing. These are not written with capital letters. e.g. car, ocean, tea, restaurant etc.

Abstract Nouns These are used for feelings or qualities that cannot be seen or touched.
e.g. happiness, love, honesty etc.

Collective Nouns These are used to describe groups. e.g. team, school, bunch, crowd etc.

Pronouns

These are words that take the place of a noun. We can use a pronoun instead of a noun.
e.g. he, you, ours, mine, yours etc.

Types of Pronouns

Following are the types of pronouns

Personal Pronouns They take the place of common and proper nouns
e.g. I, me, us, we, you, she, he, him, her, it, they, them etc.

Relative Pronouns They relate subordinate clauses to the rest of a sentence.
e.g. That, which, who, whom, whose, whichever, whoever, whomever etc.

Demonstrative Pronouns They represent a thing or a number of things.
e.g. This, these, that, those etc.

Indefinite Pronouns They refer to something not known.
e.g. All, any, most, several, none, few, both, each, anybody, anything, either, something etc.

Reflexive Pronouns These end in -self or -selves.
e.g. Myself, yourself, himself, herself, itself, ourselves, themselves, yourselves etc.

Interrogative Pronouns These are used to ask questions. e.g. What, who, which, whom, whose

Possessive Pronouns These are used to show ownership.
e.g. My, your, his, her, its, our, your, their, mine, yours, hers, ours, theirs

Subject and Object Pronouns These are used as either the subject or object in a sentence.
e.g. I, he, she, they, you, we *and* it (subject pronouns). Me, his, her, them, you, us *and* it (object pronouns).

Practice Centre

Exercise I

Choose the appropriate nouns from the options given to complete the sentences.

1. I would like to have a .... of coffee, please
- a plate
- b piece
- c cup
- d sip

2. Which .... do you like to play with, Sudha?
- a city
- b field
- c doll
- d room

3. Ravi's favourite .... in school was arithmetic.
- a subject
- b classroom
- c blackboard
- d classmate

4. Kavita left her .... at 8 o'clock to catch the bus to go to school.
- a school
- b college
- c home
- d tree

5. If you want to eat a ...., the banana is the most nutritious.
- a sweetmeat
- b fruit
- c vegetable
- d dish

6. The .... was attended by guests from both the bride's and groom's families.
- a school
- b wedding
- c picnic
- d village

7. The chain of my .... became loose, due to which I had to stop pedalling and put it back again.
- a bicycle
- b shirt
- c book
- d home

8. I've just filled forty .... of petrol in the car.
- a kilos
- b litres
- c boxes
- d metres

9. We need .... to help us when we run into problems.
- a birds
- b friends
- c animals
- d cars

10. Jamshed left his .... to find work in the nearby town.
- a chimney
- b certificate
- c village
- d toys

Exercise II

From the options given, find the noun corresponding to the word given in capitals.

1. FAIL
- a Failed
- b Failure
- c Failness
- d Fallen

2. STRIKE
- a Striking
- b Strikeners
- c Stroke
- d Stricken

3. PROPOSE
- a Proposal
- b Proposing
- c Proposed
- d Proposeness

4. OMIT
- a Omitted
- b Omitness
- c Omission
- d Omitners

5. EFFICIENT
- a Efficientness
- b Efficiency
- c Efficacy
- d Efficience

6. PAINT
- a Painters
- b Paintment
- c Painting
- d Paint

7. COLLABORATE
- a Collaborated
- b Collaboratement
- c Collaboration
- d Collaborateners

8. REFUSE
- a Refusal
- b Refuseness
- c Refusement
- d Refulat

9. MEET
- a Meety
- b Meeting
- c Meetness
- d Meetment

10. DECIDE
- a Decisiveness
- b Decision
- c Decideness
- d Decided

Exercise III

Select all the Proper Nouns in the given sentences from the given options.

1. Is John coming to the dance?
   - a John
   - b Dance
   - c John, dance
   - d None of these

2. John invited Marie and Don to the Zoo.
   - a John, Marie
   - b John, Marie, Don
   - c John, Marie, Don, Zoo
   - d None of the above

3. Carol and I went to the beach.
   - a Carol
   - b I
   - c Carol, I
   - d None of these

4. The city of Buffalo sponsored this free art show.
   - a Buffalo
   - b Art show
   - c Show
   - d None of these

5. Maria does not like this location.
   - a Location
   - b Maria
   - c Maria, location
   - d None of the above

6. Rose, Jeff and I went to see the new Science lab.
   - a Rose, Jeff, I
   - b Ross, Jeff, I, Science lab
   - c Rose, Jeff
   - d None of the above

7. Sharda does not like certain brands.
   - a Sharda, brands
   - b Certain brands
   - c Sharda
   - d None of these

8. Professor Smith teaches English to John.
   - a Professor, College, John
   - b Professor Smith, English, John
   - c Professor Smith, English
   - d None of the above

9. Jane and her friends are going to the beach.
   - a Jane
   - b Friends
   - c Jane, friends, beach
   - d None of these

10. The car that was driven by Mudit was stolen last week.
    - a Car
    - b Mudit
    - c Car, Mudit
    - d None of these

Exercise IV

Find the category of noun asked from the options given below each question.

1. Which of the following noun is a Proper Noun?
   - a Singer
   - b Peter
   - c Milk
   - d Sister

2. Which of the following is a Common Noun?
   - a Peacocks
   - b London
   - c Iron
   - d India

3. Which of the following is a Collective Noun?
   - a Team
   - b Book
   - c Marbles
   - d Ships

4. Which of the following is not an Abstract Noun?
   - a Goodness
   - b Bravery
   - c Family
   - d Childhood

5. Family is a .... Noun.
   - a Collective
   - b Abstract
   - c Concrete
   - d Countable

6. Which of the following is not a Countable Noun?
   - a Apple
   - b Horse
   - c Gold
   - d Books

7. Which of the following is not a Proper Noun?
   - a Team
   - b London
   - c Monday
   - d Nelson

8. I saw a <u>bunch</u> of grapes. The underlined word is ....
   - a Common noun
   - b Material noun
   - c Collective noun
   - d Abstract noun

9. <u>Birds</u> fly in the sky. The underlined word is a
   - a Proper noun
   - b Common noun
   - c Abstract noun
   - d Collective noun

10. Which of the following is an abstract noun?
    - a New Delhi
    - b King
    - c Army
    - d Kindness

Exercise V

Choose the correct options to fill in the blanks. In all questions, the options are
(a) he (b) she (c) it (d) they.

1. Susan is from the United States. ...... speaks English.

2. Pummy and Simi are friends. ...... are in a party.

3. Dinesh is in the street. ...... has got an Umbrella.

4. Peter has got a dog. ...... is brown in colour.

5. Tommy and Bobby are dogs. ...... are angry.

6. Sumit has got a radio. ...... is new.

7. Sheila is my friend. ...... cooks delicious food.

8. Manju has to be careful, ... can fall down.

9. The F_1 cars are very good. ...... run very fast.

10. The Delhi team wins every match because ...... is very strong.

Exercise VI

Choose the correct pronoun to complete the sentence from the options given.

1. That blue and grey saree is ....
   a me b mine c myself d yourself

2. Is this jacket ....?
   a yours b your's c yourself d mine

3. No. It is not ....
   a my b mine c yourself d me

4. .... programme was the best.
   a They're b Their c You d Mine

5. Don't be scared of .... dog.
   a our b ours
   c mine d your

6. .... bark is worse than its bite.
   a It's b Its c His d Her

7. Rohit made this T-Shirt ....
   a herself b himself c hisself d yourself

8. I wrote this poem. This poem book is not ....
   a you b yours c him d her

9. Ali and David collected the stickers ....
   a yourself b themselves
   c himself d theirself

10. Kalpana, did you write this book .... ?
    a yourself b herself c myself d self

Exercise VII

Choose the appropriate pronouns from the options given to complete the sentences.

1. Hello Harish, Kavita and Praveen. Help ...... to some food and I'll be with you in a moment.
   a you b yours
   c yourself d yourselves

2. A student of ...... has just been to see me.
   a your b yours c yourself d you

3. Manish's parents were in Mangalore. So were ....
   a mine b your c my d myself

4. The dog caught ...... tail in the door when it closed.
   a it's b itself c its d it

5. When Sunanda won the lottery, she pinched ...... to make sure she wasn't dreaming.
   a hers b herself
   c her d himself

6. ...... in the village went to the wedding but ...... enjoyed it much because of the poor arrangements.
   a Someone, no one b Nobody, no one
   c Everyone, nobody d Everyone, somebody

7. Vajpayee is .... who I have always admired.
   a someone b no one c everyone d anyone

8. You mustn't blame .... You are yourself guilty.
   a yourself b me c myself d you

9. Almost no friend of ...... came to the funeral.
   a her b myself c theirs d them

10. It's partly finished. There is ...... left.
    a nothing b everything
    c anything d something

Chapter 2

Prepositions

A preposition is a word or phrase usually placed before a noun or pronoun. It indicates its relationship to a verb or an adjective or another noun or pronoun.

Some examples of prepositions are in, at, on, during, after, until, on, in, before, by, near, up, with, by, for, of, from, through etc.

Types of Preposition

There are five types of prepositions. *These are*

1. **Prepositions of Time**   Prepositions used to denote time, are called prepositions of time. Examples are *in, on, at* etc.

    e.g. I went there *in* the evening.
    - Here, *in* is a preposition of time as it mentions the time i.e. *evening*.

    e.g. Rajat met Sameer *at* 6 o'clock.
    - In this sentence, *at* is a preposition of time as it is used to mention the time *6 o'clock*.

2. **Prepositions of Place**   Prepositions used to denote the relation of an object to its place are called as prepositions of place. Examples are *in, on, at, under, upon* etc.

    e.g. The dish is *on* the table.
    - In the sentence, *on* is a preposition of place as it tells us about the object *dish*.

    e.g. Amit is *in* the shop.
    - Here, *in* is a preposition of place as it is used to denote the place where Amit is, i.e. *shop*.

3. **Prepositions of Direction**   Prepositions used to describe a direction between two nouns are called as prepositions of direction. Examples are *to, towards, through, into* etc.

    e.g. Rita is going *towards* Ram.
    - Here, *towards* refers to a particular direction that is towards Ram.

    e.g. Sam jumped *into* the water.
    - Here, the preposition *into* points to the direction of *water*.

4. **Prepositions used for Agent**   Prepositions used to denote a thing which is the cause of another thing in the sentence. Examples are *by, with* etc.

    e.g. The book is written *by* Amit.
    - Here, the preposition *by* shows that *Amit* is the cause (Agent) for the book.

    e.g. The work was done *by* him.
    - Here, the preposition *by* joins the words *work* and *him*. It shows that *him* is cause (Agent) of the work.

5. **Prepositions used for Instrument, Device or Machine**   Prepositions used with different devices and instruments. Examples are *by, with, on* etc.

    e.g. Ram goes to school *by* bus.
    - Here, *by* is used with *bus*.

    e.g. Salim knows how to work *with* computers.
    - Here, *with* is used with *computers*. So, it is a preposition used for a device.

Practice Centre

Exercise I

Prepositions of Time

Fill in the blanks with a preposition by selecting the correct option

1. All students must reach the school _________ 9 AM to be marked present.
   - a on
   - b of
   - c before
   - d in

2. The Empire State Building in New York was completed _________ 1936.
   - a during
   - b on
   - c (no preposition)
   - d in

3. We all saw Sarita in the stadium _________ yesterday.
   - a on
   - b (no preposition)
   - c in
   - d at

4. All children prepare for attending school _________ the end _________ June.
   - a at, of
   - b on, of
   - c of, in
   - d in, for

5. Prakash told him about the accident _________ the following day.
   - a at
   - b (no preposition)
   - c in
   - d of

6. Sameer joined the team _________ the middle _________ this year.
   - a in, of
   - b of, in
   - c at, for
   - d for, of

7. All must hand in the completed project _________ 15th March.
   - a at
   - b during
   - c in
   - d on

8. We are allowed to watch cartoons on TV _________ Sundays only.
   - a in
   - b on
   - c of
   - d at

9. Karim is not at home _________ the moment.
   - a (no preposition)
   - b on
   - c at
   - d in

10. The variety programme in school starts _________ 4 PM.
    - a during
    - b at
    - c in
    - d on

Exercise II

Prepositions of Place

Fill in the blanks with a preposition by selecting the correct option:

1. Shall we all go _________ to play cricket?
   - a outside
   - b under
   - c in
   - d beyond

2. Sameera jumped _________ the fence very easily.
   - a beneath
   - b into
   - c onto
   - d above

3. I went _________ Darjeeling for a very enjoyable holiday.
   - a from
   - b to
   - c between
   - d under

4. The President lives _________ Rashtrapati Bhawan.
   - a behind
   - b in
   - c besides
   - d below

5. Is Harish going _________ the gate of the school?
   - a on
   - b below
   - c outside
   - d above

6. Take the first turning _________ the right to reach my home.
   - a to
   - b by
   - c at
   - d with

7. Anil's dog hid _______ the bed when the crackers started bursting during Diwali.

   a above   b out
   c beneath   d to

8. The cow was sleeping _______ the cowshed.

   a below   b above
   c in   d on

9. Binod and Karun cycled _______ the road for half an hour.

   a between   b under
   c in   d along

10. After finishing his work _______ Mumbai Jagdish went _______ Pune.

   a in, over   b at, to
   c over, by   d at, for

Exercise III

Prepositions Used after some Adjectives, Verbs or Nouns

Fill in the blanks with a preposition by selecting the correct option:

1. Hitler exercised complete authority _______ his followers.

   a for   b of
   c over   d in

2. Mohit has a reputation _______ honesty.

   a for   b in
   c of   d at

3. He fell a victim _______ his own greed.

   a at   b of
   c to   d from

4. I am fed up _______ him for his addiction to smoking.

   a with   b for
   c at   d on

5. Kulwant is not eligible _______ admission _______ this course because he is underage.

   a of, for   b to, for
   c for, to   d on, to

6. Obama has the stature _______ being a great teacher.

   a in   b of
   c to   d for

7. Kartik takes no interest _______ studies.

   a about   b in
   c with   d to

8. Let's proceed _______ the work in hand.

   a with   b on
   c from   d to

9. The victims _______ swine flu were mostly poor people.

   a in   b with
   c to   d of

10. The government supplied provisions and clothes _______ the victims of the flood.

   a with   b in
   c on   d to

Exercise IV

Prepositions Used in Certain Phrases

Fill in the blanks with a preposition by selecting the correct option:

1. If Papa turns ______ my request for a bicycle as a birthday present, I will be heartbroken.

   a down   b in
   c up   d at

2. If you call ______ your trip to the village, your grandmother will be unhappy.

   a on   b in
   c up   d off

3. Kavita, do not put ______ your exam preparation any longer, otherwise you will fail.

   a on   b off
   c up   d at

4. William should take ______ the task as a challenge to his abilities.

   a for   b in
   c up   d at

5. Charan, you should ring ____ the electric company to tell them about the power failure.

    a at   b up   c in   d on

6. The old bus broke ______ before it reached the bus terminus.

    a off   b in   c on   d down

7. Anyone can put ______ a small fire using a bucket of water.

    a on   b in   c up   d out

8. Don't cover ______ your mistake by telling lies.

    a on   b in   c up   d at

9. Did the foreign company take ______ Prasoon for the Branch Manager's job?

    a on   b in   c up   d at

10. The Police is entrusted ________ special powers.

    a on   b in   c with   d at

Exercise V

Story Completion with Prepositions

Fill in the blanks with suitable prepositions in the story from the options given below:

At the Garage

Customer	Have you had a chance **1.** ____ look **2.** ____ my car yet?
Mechanic	Yes, we've given it a complete examination **3.** ____ our computerised testing machine.
Customer	And what do you think is wrong **4.** ____ it?
Mechanic	That's a bit **5.** ____ a difficult answer **6.** ____ give **7.** ____ a few words.
Customer	Well, just give me a general picture **8.** ____ the problem.
Mechanic	To start **9.** ____, it's losing a lot **10.** ____ oil.
Customer	I understand. **11.** ____ this, is anything else wrong **12.** ____ it?
Mechanic	Well, there's a lot more. I mean the petrol tank has a hole **13.** ____ it.
Customer	Why don't you tell me the truth? What should be done **14.** ____ setting it right?
Mechanic	Okay, I'll come straight **15** ____ the point; you **16.** ____ buy a new car!

Options

1.   a in   b to   c (none)   d of

2.   a for   b to   c at   d in

3.   a with   b at   c for   d of

4.   a to   b in   c of   d with

5.   a for   b of   c in   d over

6.   a to   b under   c in   d of

7.   a at   b of   c for   d in

8.   a for   b at   c of   d by

9.   a of   b in   c with   d at

10.   a besides   b with   c for   d of

11.   a Apart from   b For   c In   d On

12.   a with   b in   c of   d (none)

13.   a (none)   b in   c at   d for

14.   a to   b for   c of   d in

15.   a besides   b of   c to   d in

16.   a without   b with   c at   d ought to

Chapter 3

Determiners

Determiners are words that modify nouns. In other words, determiners are the words that can be used before a noun to determine or to fix its meaning.

Types of Determiners

The common types of determiners are

1. **Article** Articles are specifically three in number, these are *a, an* and *the*. They are used to determine specific things about the subject.

   Examples of the uses of articles are
   - What *a* beautiful shot!
   - Give me *the* book.
   - I saw *an* eagle in the zoo today.

2. **Quantifier** These are used to measure the quantity of a subject. They may not specifically tell the exact amount. e.g. *few, much, many, a few, little, enough.*

   Examples of the uses of quantifiers are
   - Diksha has *enough* money to buy a guitar.
   - Dinesh wishes to have *many* players in his team.

3. **Demonstrative** These are specifically used to point at and identify the subject. e.g. *this, these, that* and *those.*

   Examples of the uses of demonstratives are
   - *This* is a glass.
   - *That* garden is really beautiful.
   - *Those* trees are very old.

4. **Possessive** These are used to show the relation between subjects. e.g. *my, our, your, his, her, their* etc.

   Examples of the uses of possessives are
   - *Their* paintings are really nice.
   - *My* classroom is very large.
   - *Her* desk is always full of books.

Practice Centre

Exercise I
Use of Articles – The, An, A

In each of the questions given below, select the correction option to fill in the blanks (some questions have more than one blank). In all questions, the options are (a) the (b) an (c) a (d) (none). The 'none' option in brackets means that no article is required.

1. Ashok is _____ quiet when he's working.

2. ____ new student has joined in our class today.

3. Wasim usually reaches _____ bus stand at about nine o'clock.

4. There is still _____ hour for _____ train to arrive.

5. Which juice is _____ more delicious - apple juice or orange juice?

6. My brother has just bought _____ flat.

7. I went to _____ bed early last night but I still feel sleepy.

8. When you enter _____ hall, you will see my sofa set.

9. When I wake up in ____ morning, I feel fresh.

10. _____ work that Yashwant is doing at _____ moment sounds boring.

11. Devesh is at _____ home now.

12. She bought _____ toy with wheels.

13. I read _____ lot of books on _____ scientists and this one is best.

14. Let us go into town _____later. I'd like to do some shopping.

15. _____ town where my grandmother lives is very pretty.

16. _____ air is cleanest in _____ morning. It's too dirty at evening time.

17. He is always in _____ hurry to go home.

18. Savita is _____ idiot to have failed such _____ simple test.

19. Of all _____ people in our office, Arvind is _____ calmest.

20. ____ apple ____ day keeps _____ doctor away.

Exercise II
Use of Demonstratives That, This, These and Those

In the questions given below, select the correct option to fill in the blank. In all questions, the options are (a) that (b) this (c) these (d) those. The phrase given in brackets in some questions gives you a hint of the answer.

1. (Talking about a book in your hand) How could you buy something like _____?

2. The jeans you have bought today are better than _____ you bought last month.

3. (With a bowl full of grapes on your lap) _____ grapes are delicious!

4. (pointing to the computer) Raghu never uses _____ computer.

5. (About a picture you've just taken from your purse) _____ is my wife.

6. Could you bring me _____ book I left in the garden?

7. (Pointing to the birds) _____ birds sing in _____ tree every morning.

8. Many parents complain about their children _____ days.

9. Waiter, I'm sorry to say it but _____ soup you have just served me is awful.

10. (During a long walk) I should have worn _____ shoes I bought in Agra last year; _____ have never been comfortable.

Exercise III

Use of Possessives

Replace the pronouns (in brackets) with adjectives from the options given.

1. Kareena loves (she) ______ pet cat very much.
- a her
- b its
- c my
- d his

2. Anil goes to school in the bus with (he) ______ sister.
- a their
- b our
- c her
- d his

3. (You) ______ name is Lakshman, isn't it?
- a Your
- b Our
- c Her
- d Its

4. Here is (we) ______ professor.
- a our
- b their
- c your
- d his

5. (I) ______ husband and I want to go to Mumbai.
- a Mine
- b My
- c Yours
- d Her

6. Where is (I) ______ school bag?
- a theirs
- b its
- c my
- d our

7. We went to Agra to see ______ historical monuments.
- a their
- b its
- c her
- d our

8. (You) ______ laptop is very expensive.
- a My
- b Your
- c Mine
- d Theirs

9. (You) ______ favourite hobby is collecting matchbox labels.
- a Mine
- b Yours
- c Your
- d Its

10. (They) ____ father works in the government.
- a Its
- b Their
- c Her
- d His

Exercise IV

Use of Quantifiers

Fill in the blanks with quantifiers from the options given. Hints are given in [ ] after many questions to guide you.

1. In London in the winter there's hardly ______ sunlight.
- a some
- b any
- c many
- d few

2. Could you give me ______ your time and your money? [A request – I expect you will say 'yes'.]
- a each
- b little
- c enough
- d both

3. Did you buy ______ butter? [I expect you will say 'yes', because we talked about it before.]
- a some
- b any
- c little
- d less

4. ______ and ______ one of you is to blame for our team losing the final. [Coach is talking to the players after a match.]
- a Some, many
- b Every, each
- c Each, every
- d Many, enough

5. Varun, I found ______ mistakes in your answer paper. [A large number]
- a many
- b whole
- c some
- d any

6. Go into ______ shop in the market and ask; you will get it.[it doesn't matter which shop]
- a all
- b few
- c many
- d any

7. ______ student will tell you that they don't have ______ money. [it doesn't matter which student]
- a Each, enough
- b Every, less
- c Any, enough
- d Few, much

8. Can I have ______ more juice? [I expect you will say 'yes'.]
- a all
- b much
- c some
- d little

9. Did you buy ______ tomato sauce? [I have no idea, this is a real question.]
- a much
- b any
- c enough
- d whole

10. Would you like to eat ______ more rice? [An offer – I think you will say 'yes'.]
- a many
- b few
- c enough
- d some

Chapter 4

Conjunctions

Conjunctions are used to join two or more sentences, words or phrases.

There are four kinds of conjunctions

1. **Co-ordinating Conjunctions**
   These are used to join two parts of a sentence that are grammatically equal. The two parts may be single words or clauses.
   e.g. *for, and, nor, but, or, yet, so* etc.

2. **Correlative Conjunctions**
   These are used in pairs.
   e.g. *not only .... but also, either .... or, neither .... nor, although .... yet* etc.

3. **Subordinate Conjunctions**
   These are used to join together a dependent clause and a main clause.
   e.g. *when, since, as, before, after, until, unless, if that, so that, provided that, because, till* etc.

4. **Compound Conjunctions**
   These are phrases used to join together two or more clauses.
   e.g. *as if, in order to, as soon as, as well as, even if* etc.

Practice Centre

Exercise I
Coordinating Conjunctions

Fill in the blanks with suitable Coordinating Conjunctions from the options given.

1. Hema Malini is a graceful dancer _____ people enjoy watching her.

   a or   b nor   c and   d but

2. Did Lalit phone you in the afternoon _____ in the evening?

   a but   b nor   c yet   d or

3. Other actors try to imitate Amitabh's style of acting, _____ they have not succeeded.

   a and   b yet   c for   d so

4. Salman is talented, _____ he will attract fans for many years to come.

   a nor   b for   c yet   d so

5. Sachin didn't take any coaching, _____ did he need to.

   a nor   b or   c but   d yet

6. Chris Gayle's batting technique is unconventional, _____ the effect is striking.

   a for   b but   c nor   d or

7. Spectators love to watch football, ____ it is a very fast game.
   a yet
   b but
   c for
   d or

8. Parul lost her balance on the stool ____ she did not fall.
   a and
   b so
   c or
   d but

9. Dhoni is such a player that he can fill an audience with joy ____ he can bring people to tears.
   a for
   b so
   c but
   d or

10. Satish didn't want help, ____ did he ask for it.
   a but
   b nor
   c yet
   d so

Exercise II

Subordinating Conjunctions

Fill in the blanks with suitable Subordinating Conjunctions from the options given.

1. Several homes burned down ____ a gas pipeline exploded.
   a because
   b unless
   c until
   d till

2. ____ the firemen arrived quickly, they could not stop the fire from spreading.
   a After
   b Since
   c Even if
   d Though

3. He asked ____ I needed an umbrella.
   a if only
   b than
   c if
   d so that

4. Karim went to jail ____ pay the fine for ticketless travel.
   a although
   b rather than
   c before
   d wherever

5. ____ she was cooking the dinner, her baby went to sleep.
   a Where
   b As though
   c While
   d Before

6. ____ you called, he picked up the phone immediately.
   a When
   b As long as
   c Whereas
   d Even though

7. We can sit in the park for ____ we want.
   a yet
   b but
   c for
   d as long as

8. The dog didn't go outside ____ it rained.
   a if only
   b when
   c that
   d as if

9. ____ the cook smelled gas leaking from the cylinder, he did not warn the children to run out of the house.
   a In order that
   b Now that
   c Even though
   d Since

10. ____ it was raining, he continued walking.
   a So that
   b If only
   c Where
   d Though

Exercise III

Correlative Conjunctions

Fill in the blanks with Correlative Conjunctions from the options given. Some sentences may have more than one correct answer.

1. ____ Pradeep ____ Suresh wants to lose, as they are very competitive.
   a Both, and
   b Neither, nor
   c Not, but
   d Whether, or

2. Sarita is ____ fond of animals ____ Rubina is.
   a whether, or
   b not, but
   c as, as
   d both, and

3. ____ does our teacher encourage us to work hard, ____ she praises us when we succeed.
   a Not only, but also
   b Either, or
   c Whether, or
   d Not, but

4. ____ Alok will become an engineer ____ a lawyer, he's not sure yet.
   a Whether, or
   b Neither, nor
   c Both, and
   d Not only, but also

5. Kapil is ____ very athletic in build, ____ his brother is.

   a both, and
   b not, but
   c whether, or
   d either, nor

6. Every term, ____ Madhu ____ Manju do very well in class.

   a not, but
   b both, and
   c whether, or
   d either, or

7. ____ my brother ____ my sister are doctors.

   a Whether, or
   b Not, but
   c Both, and
   d Not, and

8. Last month, ____ did Vijay get the first position in class, ____ he won the 'Best Athlete' award.

   a both, and
   b not, but
   c whether, or
   d not only, but also

9. ____ Shakeel ____ Vinod are weak students.

   a Whether, or
   b Both, and
   c Not, but
   d Not, and

10. ____ my sister ____ I want to attend Dinesh's birthday party, as we don't like him.

   a Either, or
   b Not, but
   c Neither, nor
   d Whether, or

Exercise IV

Mixed Exercise on Conjunctions

Fill in the blanks with suitable conjunctions from the options given. Some blanks may have more than one correct answer.

1. Karun waited ________ his sister Manju woke up, as he was not in a hurry to go out.

   a as   b unless
   c but   d until

2. ________ you're here, we will let you in on a secret.

   a Unless   b Nor
   c Either   d Now that

3. Lalit has a very clear idea about what career he wants, ________ Mohit is having no idea about his career.

   a because   b unless
   c while   d till

4. Ravinder is very good at writing essays, ________ Pankaj is good at Science.

   a so that   b both
   c whether   d while

5. Srilata told the interviewers that she wanted the job badly, ________ she didn't have the required qualifications.

   a as though
   b although
   c till
   d nor

6. Ramesh's family had their dinner early ________ then watched KBC on TV.

   a and   b till
   c nor   d though

7. Akshara likes to do her work in advance; ________, Abhishek does his work at the last minute.

   a because   b however
   c as long as   d both

8. ____ Puneet is very organised and neat, Yashwant is disorganised and drops his things everywhere.

   a Whereas   b Unless
   c But   d Until

9. Sameer stayed at home ________ it was raining heavily.

   a both   b Even though
   c because   d whereas

10. ________ Nikhil claims that he is innocent, everyone knows he is guilty.

   a Because
   b Even though
   c While
   d Till

Exercise V

Story Completion with Conjunctions

Fill in the blanks with suitable connectors in the story given below from the options given.

It was a very cloudy and windy day. **1.** _______, we went sailing on the sea. We took our wind-breaker jackets **2.** _______ the weather was chilly. It's best not to eat much before sailing **3.** _______ we may be hungry. We take lots of bottled water to drink **4.** _______ we get thirsty while sailing. You can bring your lunch on board **5.** _______ you get seasick.

Experienced sailors are better at guiding the boat over rough water. **6.** _______, novice sailors are more patient when bringing the ship back to port. One time when we were passing under the harbour bridge and going out to sea, a huge wave turned the ship on its side. **7.** _______, we had to call for assistance. **8.** _______ there is an emergency, we have a radio and life raft. We've had very few problems, **9.** _______ some close calls with other boats. **10.** _______ there are boating rules, not everyone follows them.

Options

1.	a Consequently	b Even though	**6.**	a Nevertheless	b Otherwise
	c In spite of	d Nevertheless		c Therefore	d However
2.	a even though	b despite	**7.**	a Otherwise	b Since
	c since	d due to		c Consequently	d Nevertheless
3.	a because	b even though	**8.**	a If	b Only if
	c provided that	d despite		c But	d Unless
4.	a also	b because	**9.**	a yet	b despite
	c otherwise	d consequently		c because of	d even though
5.	a since	b as long as	**10.**	a Since	b Even though
	c unless	d providing that		c In spite of	d But

Chapter 5

Modals

Modals are a type of auxiliary (helping) verbs that are used to express ability, possibility, permission or obligation. They are used with verbs to exhibit different characteristics. They can express different meanings in different contexts.

Some commonly used modals are *can, could, will, would, shall, should, may, might, need, need not, ought to, had better* etc.

Uses of Modals

Examples of the use of some modals in different sentences are

- Heena *can* swim.
- It *may* rain tomorrow!
- You *should* take an umbrella. It's starting to rain.
- I *might* go on holiday to England next year.
- *Could* I use your comb, please?
- *Shall* I order a pizza?
- You *ought to* revise your lessons.
- Tomorrow I *will* be in Delhi.

Notes
1. *Can* and *may* are used to express permission. *May* is rather formal and polite.
2. *Shall* is used in first person and *will* in all persons to express future. Nowadays *shall* is less commonly used than *will*.
3. *Could* and *might* are used as less positive versions of *can* and *may*.

Practice Centre

Exercise I
Modal Verbs of Ability / Obligation / Necessity / Advice

Choose the right modal verb from the options given to fill in the blanks.

1. As we are in a hospital, you _________ smoke cigarettes.
   a must not   b may not   c don't have to   d need not

2. You _________ take your sun goggles, as it is cloudy.
   a could not   b may not   c need not   d must not

3. People _________ not walk on the lawn.
   a need   b may   c could   d must

4. Cars on the road _________ stop when the traffic lights are red.
   a could   b need   c may   d must

5. You _______ leave small plastic items lying around, as such objects _____ be swallowed by infants.

    a need not, must   b need, need

    c may not, may   d should not, may

6. There is enough milk in the refrigerator. You _______ not buy any more.

    a need   b could

    c may   d must

7. Carry an umbrella with you, as it _______ rain later.

    a need   b must not

    c should   d might

8. Reena: "_______ you stand on your head for more than five minutes?"

Meena: "No, I _______."

    a Need, needn't   b Must, mustn't

    c Can, can't   d May, mayn't

9. Devesh has been awake for more than 24 hours. He _______ get some sleep.

    a would   b may

    c had better   d must

10. If you want to learn to speak English fluently, you _____ to talk with everyone in English only.

    a must not   b need not

    c need   d could

Exercise II

Modal Verbs of Logical Assumption / Possibility / Probability / Request

Choose the right modal verb from the options given to fill in the blanks.

1. Why is that tall woman looking around like that? She _______ surely be lost.

    a can't   b might   c must   d could

2. When anyone is driving very slowly on an empty road, he _______ surely be talking on his mobile phone.

    a must   b need   c can't   d might

3. Polar bears _______ be starving, as there is a lot of fish available for them.

    a might   b could   c can't   d must

4. Anil _______ have much money or he would buy a new car. His earlier car is in very poor condition.

    a can't   b may   c could   d might

5. _______ you smoke outside, please?

    a May   b Might   c Can't   d Could

6. Parikshit couldn't find his spectacles. He thought he _______ have left them at the office.

    a may   b must   c might   d can't

7. Before this year end, I _________ move out of my parents' house because I do not have a job.

    a might   b may   c must   d can't

8. There _______ be something wrong with the fan! It's making a very unusual noise.

    a must   b can   c can't   d could

9. It takes only one and a half hours to drive down from Delhi to Agra? That _______ be correct!

    a must   b can't   c may   d can

10. Roli and Puneeta _______ be drinking a lot of tea. They've finished two packets this month.

    a must   b could   c can   d can't

Exercise III

Modal Verbs (Mixed)

Fill in the blanks from the options given using the verb given in brackets after the blank as a hint.

1. Wasim, if you needed money, you _________ (ask) me instead of asking your mother.

    a may have asked   b couldn't have asked

    c should have asked   d can't have asked

2. "How is the electrician getting on?" "He _________ (finish) the wiring – I'll go and see."

    a need have finished   b could have finished

    c may have finished   d can't have finished

3. You _________ (put) so much chillies in the sambhar; I'm not able to eat it.

    a must not have put   b need not have put

    c could not have put   d can't have put

4. Rajesh never got my letter, as I _________ (address) it properly.

    a must have addressed   b could have addressed

    c can have addressed   d mustn't have addressed

5. "Karuna is not here." "Surely she _________ (forget) – I reminded her yesterday."
   a can't have forgotten   b could have forgotten
   c can have forgotten   d must have forgotten

6. I _________ (find) a new house to live in – I'll know tomorrow after talking to the owner.
   a must have found   b have found
   c can have found   d may have found

7. I did not have enough money for the bus ticket, so I _________ (walk) to my home.
   a should have walked   b could have walked
   c had to walk   d may have walked

8. The Sandhu family is not at home, because they _________ (go) away for a holiday.
   a can't have gone   b may have gone
   c will not have gone   d shouldn't have gone

9. When Chandran abused Kiran loudly, Kiran _________ (kill) him.
   a can't have killed   b must have killed
   c can have killed   d could have killed

10. Gauri _________ (phone) you, but she didn't have your number.
   a should have phoned   b must have phoned
   c may have phoned   d need not have phoned

Exercise IV

Identification of the Correct Modals in a Story

Fill in the blanks in the dialogue from the options given below.

Girdhari I know this is "last minute", but **1.** _____ you come with us to a party this evening?

Savitri Well, I don't know. I **2.** _________ be able to come.

Girdhari I know that I **3.** _________ you two days ago, but it slipped my mind.

Savitri That happens to me too. You **4.** _________ preoccupied with your work.

Girdhari Yes, last week was a little tough. I **5.** _______a report ready for my boss. It took quite some time. After several attempts, I **6.** _________the report together.

Savitri If you'd like, I **7.** ______ read your report and give you feedback.

Girdhari Thanks, that **8.** _________ helpful. **9.** _______ I show it to you?

Savitri That's a good idea. Then I **10.** ______ to get an idea how brilliant you are.

Savitri (after reading the report) This is really good, Girdhari! It **11.** _________ you a long time to do.

Girdhari It **12.** _________ only a few hours, but instead it took me two afternoons to prepare.

Savitri Well, it shows. It **13.** _________ your boss.

Girdhari I hope so. I **14.** _______ have to present it the day after tomorrow at noon.

Savitri Great! **15.** _________ go to the party now?

Girdhari Let's go!

1.	a shall	b may	c can	d might
2.	a can't	b must	c could	d might
3.	a should tell	b may have told	c can't have told	d should have told
4.	a must be	b must have been	c can't have been	d might have
5.	a had to get	b must have gotten	c need to get	d might get
6.	a can't put	b was able to put	c could able to put	d might put
7.	a can't	b may	c could	d might
8.	a can't be	b would be	c must be	d might be
9.	a Can't	b Shall	c Will	d Might
10.	a can't be able	b may able	c could able	d would be able
11.	a can't take	b must have taken	c must take	d might have taken
12.	a can't have taken	b may take	c could take	d should have taken
13.	a might impress	b can't impress	c should impress	d should have impressed
14.	a can't	b may	c won't	d will
15.	a Shall we	b May we	c Could we	d Might be

Chapter 6

Tenses

It is a grammatical reference to time in a sentence. It indicates the time when the situation or event took place. *Basically, tenses are divided into three broad categories:*

1. Any event or situation that happens now is said to be in the **present tense**. e.g. Raman plays chess.

2. Any event or situation that happened before now is said to be in the **past tense**. e.g. Raman played chess in the morning.

3. Any event or situation that will happen after now is said to be in the **future tense**. e.g. Raman will play chess on Monday.

Types of Tenses

The three categories of tenses are further divided into four types each:

1. **Simple Present Tense**   It is used to denote an event, without anything being said about the completeness or incompleteness of the event.
   e.g. *Rajat plays.*

2. **Present Continuous Tense**   It is used to denote an event which is incomplete or continuous, that is the event is still going on.
   e.g. *Rakhi is studying.*

3. **Present Perfect Tense**   It is used to denote an event that is finished, complete or perfect at the time of speaking.
   e.g. *I have studied.*

4. **Present Perfect Continuous Tense**   It is used to denote an event which is going on continuously and is not completed at the present moment.
   e.g. *I have been playing.*

5. **Simple Past Tense**   It is used to indicate an event which was completed in the past.
   e.g. *I reached Delhi yesterday.*

6. **Past Continuous Tense**   It is used to denote an event going on at sometime in the past. The time, the event happened may or may not be included.
   e.g. *It was getting darker.*

7. **Past Perfect Tense**   It describes an event completed before a certain moment in the past.
   e.g. *When I reached the station the train had started.*

8. **Past Perfect Continuous Tense**   It is used for an event that began before a certain point in the past and continued upto that time.
   e.g. *At that time, he had been writing a novel for two months.*

9. **Simple Future Tense**   It is used to express future and is about events which we cannot control.
   e.g. *I shall be twenty next Sunday.*

10. **Future Continuous Tense**   It is used to talk about events which will be in progress at a time in the future.
    e.g. *This time tomorrow I will be sitting on the bench.*

11. **Future Perfect Tense**   It is used to talk about events that will be completed by a certain time in the future.
    e.g. *I shall have written my exercise by then.*

12. **Future Perfect Continuous Tense**   It is used to denote events which will be in progress over a period of time that will end in the future.
    e.g. *I will have been working here for twenty years next June.*

Practice Centre

Exercise I
Simple Past and Present Perfect Tense

Select the correct option to fill in the blanks with either the correct Simple Past or Present Perfect Tense of the verb given in brackets after the blank.

1. Yesterday Harish and Sameer _______ (go) to the mall.
   a were going
   b went
   c will go
   d going

2. Savita ______ (just/finish) her homework.
   a will just finish
   b just finishing
   c have just finished
   d has just finished

3. Satish _______ (already / travel) to Kashmir twice during the last three years.
   a travelled already
   b has already travelled
   c have already travelled
   d already travelling

4. _______ (you / ever / see) a tiger?
   a Has you ever seen
   b You ever see
   c Have you ever seen
   d Have you ever saw

5. My cousin Milind _______ (be) in Germany five years ago.
   a will be
   b is
   c was
   d will have been

6. I _______ (not / be) to Canada so far.
   a not go
   b will not be
   c has not been
   d have not been

7. Malvika _______ (already / write) three letters.
   a has already written
   b already written
   c will already write
   d already wrote

8. _______ (they / spend) their holidays in Goa last winter?
   a They spent
   b Will they spend
   c They spending
   d Did they spend

9. Tarvinder _______ (move) to his home town in 1999.
   a has moved
   b will move
   c moved
   d moving

10. I can't take any photos because I _______ (not /buy) a new film for my Nikon camera.
   a has not bought
   b have not bought
   c not bought
   d not buy

Exercise II
Simple Future or Future Perfect Tense

Select the correct option to fill in the blanks with either the correct Simple Future or Future Perfect Tense of the verb given in brackets after the blank.

1. I think Sunil _______ (start) his journey tomorrow.
   a will start
   b will started
   c will be starting
   d have started

2. Our teacher _______ (correct) the test papers by Sunday.
   a will correct
   b will be correcting
   c will have corrected
   d correcting

3. Aditya _______ (certainly / get) good marks in the Hindi test.
   a certainly got
   b certainly is getting
   c certainly getting
   d will certainly get

4. By 6 PM, Karuna _______ (finish) her homework.
   a has finished
   b will have finished
   c is finishing
   d had finishing

5. The train _______ (leave) from Ahmedabad by 8 PM.
   a have left
   b had left
   c was leaving
   d will have left

6. My grandmother _______ (arrive) at home by now.
   a will have arrived
   b had arrived
   c will be arriving
   d arriving

7. The cricket match _________ (end) by then.
   a had ended
   b will have ended
   c will end
   d had ended

8. I think that tomorrow Raveena _________ (start) her new project.

   a starting   b is start
   c will start   d is starting

9. My class teacher _______ (probably / assign) a lot of homework for the summer holidays.
   a probably assigned
   b probably has assigned
   c probably assigning
   d will probably assign

10. The building contractor _________ (finish) my house by next month.
   a have finished   b finished
   c will have finished   d will finishing

Exercise III

All Tenses

Fill in the blanks with the correct form of the verb given in brackets after the blank by selecting the correct option. In some questions there is more than one blank.

1. Sarla's mother _____ (stay) in a rented house after her divorce.
   a will stays   b will staying
   c will be stayed   d has been staying

2. Varun ______ (bring up) by his father because his mother died when he was a baby.
   a was bringing up   b has been bring up
   c has brought up   d was brought up

3. My brother, who ______ (work) in Kolkata for 10 years, ______ (be) now seriously ill.
   a working, was
   b has been working, is
   c will be working, will be
   d has work, was

4. My mother _______ (burn) her fingers while she _______ (cook) the dinner.
   a burn, cooking   b burning, cooking
   c burnt, was cooking   d burn, cooked

5. I once _______ (hear) Honey Singh _______ (sing) live on the stage.
   a will hear, sang   b heard, singing
   c heard, sung   d had heard, sung

6. The school rules do not _______ (permit) students going outside the school during school hours.
   a permitted   b permitting
   c had permitted   d permit

7. Mihir ______ (be) my best friend. He ______ (stay) in Kanpur for five years.
   a is, has been staying   b was, will stayed
   c will be, staying   d is, had staying

8. Anamika _______ (break) her left ankle bone while she _______ (dance) at the party.
   a break, danced
   b broke, was dancing
   c was breaking, danced
   d break, danced

9. Kulwant isn't here as he just _____ (go) out.
   a gone   b will be going
   c going   d went

10. Tailor Master, are the clothes I _______ (give) for stitching ready yet?
   a will give   b giving
   c had given   d given

11. Lalita ______ (not write) a letter to me since last year.
   a not writing   b have not writing
   c has not wrote   d has not written

12. Upendra _______ (win) the wrestling bout against Vijay today, I'm sure.
   a will win   b would winning
   c has won   d won

13. Mummy, tell Papa that his phone ______ (ring) while he _______ (have) his bath.
   a was ringing, having
   b rung, had
   c rang, was having
   d was ringing, have

14. Now Rajendra ______ (want) to move to a bigger city for a better job.
   a wanting   b is wanted
   c wants   d has want

15. Balbir ______ (leave) Mumbai four years ago.
  a left
  b had leave
  c will leave
  d is leaving

16. The famous Dr Prahlad ______(operate) on my uncle tomorrow to cure his cancer.
  a will operating
  b will operate
  c operated
  d has operated

17. Our office computer operator ______(type) ten pages every day.
  a will typing
  b has typing
  c will typed
  d types

18. I would have written to Abhishek if I ______ (know) his address.
  a knew
  b had known
  c will have known
  d known

19. Mr Mazumdar ______ (undergo) treatment for the past one year for high blood pressure.
  a undergoes
  b has been undergoing
  c undergoing
  d will undergo

20. Sarita must ______ (forget) about me.
  a forgot
  b have forgotten
  c forgotten
  d have forget

Exercise IV

Mixed Tenses in a Story

Fill in the blanks with the correct form of the verb given in brackets after the blank by selecting the correct option.

One day a husband and wife **1.** ______ (drive) to the countryside to visit their friends when they realised they needed to stop for petrol. The man was filling up the car when he **2.** ______ (see) a penguin standing by the petrol pump. He **3.** ______ (think) it was very strange and when he went to the cashier to pay, he asked, "Why is there a penguin standing next to the pump?"

The cashier replied, "I don't know. It **4.** ______ (be) there all morning."

The man replied, "Well, we can't leave it there, it's too dangerous. He might have an accident. What should I do?"

The cashier **5.** ______ (suggest), "You should take it to the zoo."

"That's a good idea," the man said. "I **6.** ______ (take) him now."

So the man and his wife put the penguin in the car and **7.** ______ (drive) away. One week later, the man and his wife **8.** ______ (return) to the same petrol pump to fill petrol in the car and the penguin was still in the car. When the man went to pay, the cashier said to him, "I thought you **9.** ______ (take) the penguin to the zoo."

The man replied, "We did. The penguin had a really good time there. So tonight, we **10.** ______ (take) him to a fish restaurant."

1.
  a had driving
  b drive
  c was driving
  d were driving

6.
  a take
  b took
  c will take
  d would took

2.
  a seen
  b have saw
  c saw
  d did see

7.
  a had drove
  b has drive
  c driven
  d drove

3.
  a was think
  b thought
  c think
  d will think

8.
  a returning
  b returned
  c did return
  d have returning

4.
  a has been
  b been
  c be
  d will be

9.
  a taken
  b take
  c took
  d will take

5.
  a suggest
  b suggested
  c will suggest
  d were suggesting

10.
  a taking
  b taken
  c should take
  d are taking

Chapter 7

Active and Passive Voice

Active Voice

Sentences in active voice tell us something that a person or a thing does. In other words, the active voice expresses an action in which the subject is actively engaged. In active voice, the subject is performing the verb.

Example
The *teacher drew* the diagram on the blackboard.

Passive Voice

The passive voice tells us something that is done to a person or a thing. In other words, the subject in the passive voice is not the doer of the action but its recipient. In passive voice, the subject is receiving the verb.

Example
John was hit by a car.

Examples of Voice Transformation in Different Tenses

Tense	Active Voice	Passive Voice
Simple Present	take or takes	am taken, is taken, are taken
Present Continuous	am taking, is taking, are taking	am being taken, is being taken, are being taken
Present Perfect	has taken, have taken	has been taken, have been taken
Simple Past	took	was taken, were taken
Past Continuous	was taking, were taking	was being taken, were being taken
Past Perfect	had taken	had been taken
Simple Future	will take, shall take	will be taken, shall be taken
can/may/must/ etc + base verb	can take, must take	can be taken, must be taken

Practice Centre

Exercise I

Active and Passive Verb Forms

Fill in the blanks with suitable active or passive verb forms from the options given.

1. The injured ______ to the hospital in an ambulance.
   - a were taking
   - b was taking
   - c were taken
   - d have taken

2. Suresh ______ reading the book since yesterday.
   - a is
   - b has been
   - c have been
   - d was

3. My uncle ______ writing poems for a while.
   - a has been
   - b is
   - c are
   - d have been

4. Our Lucknow house ______ in 1990 by my father.
   - a built
   - b was built
   - c was build
   - d has built

5. Shazia and Sharmila ______ notes for the examination.
   - a have preparing
   - b been prepared
   - c had preparing
   - d are preparing

6. As grandmother could not walk, she ______ home in a wheelchair.
   - a has carried
   - b has been carried
   - c was carried
   - d was carrying

7. The criminals ______ arrested by the police.
   - a have
   - b had
   - c was
   - d have been

8. Premchand ______ to become a successful writer.
   - a had always wanted
   - b have always wanted
   - c am always wanted
   - d am always wanting

9. I ______ playing cricket for five hours.
   - a has been
   - b have been
   - c was
   - d am

10. The teacher ______ punished the student for lying.
    - a have been
    - b (no word)
    - c is
    - d was

Exercise II

Active to Passive

In each of the active voice sentences given below, a sentence with a blank space meaning the same is given in passive voice alongside. Fill in the correct words in the blank space by selecting one of the options given.

Active Voice	**Passive voice**
1. My car hit the dog on the road	The dog on the road ______ my car.
2. The dolphins had learned many tricks.	Many tricks ______ the dolphins.
3. Jagdish answered the question.	The question ______ Jagdish.
4. The mason will build the house in three months.	The house ______ the mason in three months.
5. Zimbabwe won the match against Bangladesh.	The match against Bangladesh ______ by Zimbabwe.
6. Salim cleans the office every day.	The office ______ Salim every day.
7. Somebody will meet you at the airport.	You ______ at the airport.
8. The heavy traffic must have delayed Sunil.	Sunil must have ______ the heavy traffic.
9. Shakespeare wrote many plays.	Many plays ______ Shakespeare.
10. Sunita showed her boss the new laptop.	The new laptop ______ Sunita to her boss.

Options

1.	a	hit by	b	is hitting	c	was hit by	d	is hit by
2.	a	learned by	b	is learned by	c	was learned by	d	had been learned by
3.	a	answered by	b	was answered by	c	is answering by	d	is answered by
4.	a	will be built by	b	is built by	c	was building by	d	is build by
5.	a	will be won	b	is won	c	had been won	d	were won
6.	a	cleaned by	b	is cleaned by	c	was cleaned by	d	is cleaning by
7.	a	will be met	b	is being met	c	was met	d	is met
8.	a	delayed by	b	delaying by	c	delay by	d	been delayed by
9.	a	written by	b	is written by	c	are written by	d	were written by
10.	a	showed by	b	was shown by	c	was showed by	d	is shown by

Exercise III
Passive to Active

In each of the passive voice sentences given below, a sentence with a blank space meaning the same is given in active voice alongside. Fill in the correct words in the blank space by selecting one of the options given.

Passive Voice	**Active voice**
1. The cow is fed by Mohini.	Mohini ______ the cow.
2. The letter was posted by Varun.	Varun ______ the letter.
3. Milk is delivered in the morning.	The milkman ______ in the morning.
4. A new stadium is being built by the government.	The government ______ a new stadium.
5. New cars are often stolen.	Thieves ______ new cars.
6. Kewal had been cheated by the shopkeeper.	The shopkeeper ______.
7. The spider was being killed by Amit.	Amit ______ the spider.
8. Maize is sown in the rainy season.	Farmers ______ in the rainy season.
9. A problem has been created by you.	______ a problem.
10. My friends have been invited to my party.	I ______ friends to my party.

Options

1.	a	feeding	b	is feed	c	will feed	d	feeds
2.	a	had posted	b	is posting	c	will post	d	posted
3.	a	delivering the milk	b	delivered the milk	c	delivers the milk	d	will deliver the milk
4.	a	will build	b	is building	c	was building	d	was built
5.	a	will often steal	b	often stole	c	often stealing	d	often steal
6.	a	was cheating Kewal	b	will cheat Kewal	c	had cheated Kewal	d	cheating Kewal
7.	a	will killed	b	was killing	c	was killed	d	will kill
8.	a	sow maize	b	will sow maize	c	sowing maize	d	sowed maize
9.	a	You will create	b	You create	c	You have created	d	You created
10.	a	am inviting my	b	invite my	c	invited my	d	have invited my

Exercise IV

Active and Passive Voice in a Passage

In the passage given below, fill in the blanks in the sentences by selecting one of the options from those given below the passage.

Fiat ______ **1.** by a group of Italian businessmen in 1899. In 1903, Fiat, ______ **2.** 132 cars. Some of these cars ______ **3.** by the company to the United States and Britain. In 1920, Fiat ______ **4.** making cars at a new factory at Lingotto, near Turin. There was a track on the roof where the cars ______ **5.** by technicians. In 1936, Fiat ______ **6.** the Fiat 500. This car ______ **7.** the Topolino – the Italian name for Mickey Mouse. The company grew, and in 1963 Fiat ______ **8.** more than 300000 vehicles. Today, Fiat is based in Turin and its cars ______ **9.** all over the world. They ______ **10.** for their excellent quality of manufacture.

Options

1.	a started	b was started	c was starting	d had start
2.	a produced	b was produced	c was producing	d produce
3.	a was exported	b had export	c exported	d were exported
4.	a start	b started	c was started	d starting
5.	a testing	b tested	c were tested	d were testing
6.	a has launch	b launch	c launched	d was launching
7.	a was calling	b called	c is calling	d was called
8.	a exported	b was exported	c did exporting	d exporting
9.	a sold	b are sold	c was sold	d will sold
10.	a are known	b know	c known	d are knowing

Chapter 8

Direct and Indirect Speech

Direct Speech refers to the actual words of the speaker as spoken by her/him. Indirect speech (also called reported speech) is when you tell somebody else what you or a person said before.

Types of Reported Speech

1. **When transforming statements** we should check whether we have to change *pronouns*, the *tense* or the *place, demonstratives* and *time expression*.

Example 1	She says, "My dad likes roast chicken." *will change to* She says that her dad likes roast chicken.
Example 2	He says, "I write English poems." *will be changed to* He says that he writes English poems. (*No change in tense*)
but	He said, "I am happy." *will be changed to* He said that he was happy. (*Tense is changed or shifted back*)

2. **When transforming questions** we should check whether we have to change *pronouns*, the *tense* or the *place, demonstratives* and *time expression*.

Example	He said, "Why don't you speak English?" *will change to* He asked me why I didn't speak English.

3. **When reporting requests/commands** we should check whether we have to change *pronouns* and *place* and *time expression*.

Example 1 *The command*	He said, "Nancy, do the exercise." *will change to* He told Nancy to do the exercise.
Example 2 *The request*	He said, "Nancy, please give me your pen." *will change to* He requested / asked Nancy to give him / her pen.

4. **When reporting other types of sentences** some rules to be followed are:

Example 1	He said, "You must read this book." *will change to* He advised / urged me to read that book.
Example 2 *either* *or*	He said, "Let's go to the cinema." *will change to* He suggested going to the cinema. He suggested that we should go to the cinema.
Example 3	He said, "I saw her but she didn't see me." *will change to* He said that he had seen her but she hadn't seen him.

Practice Centre

Exercise I
Direct to Indirect

Select the correct option to complete the sentence given in indirect speech in each question.In some questions there is more than one blank.

1. "I may lend you some money", promised Milind.

Milind promised that he _____ some money.

   a lend me

   b may lend you

   c might lend you

   d might lend me

2. Ramesh said, "I met you yesterday."

Ramesh told me he _____ the previous day.

   a is meeting me

   b has meet me

   c had met me

   d had meet me

3. "I cannot come", explained Mohini.

Mohini explained that _____ come.

   a she cannot

   b she could not

   c I cannot not

   d I shall not

4. Taruna said, "I have not done my assignment today."

Taruna explained that _____ done _____ assignment _____.

   a she had not, my, that day

   b she had not, her, today

   c I had not, my, today

   d she had not, her, that day

5. "I could fall down", exclaimed Kavita.

Kavita was afraid that _____ down.

   a she could fall

   b she would fall

   c I could fall

   d she falling

6. "Grandmother must rest", said the doctor.

The doctor advised grandmother _____.

   a had to rest

   b has to rest

   c must rest

   d to rest

7. "I have already replied", claimed Karan.

Karan claimed that _____ replied.

   a I had already

   b he had already

   c he already

   d I already

8. Vidya said to me, "You needn't take off your shoes in our house."

Vidya reminded me that _____ take off my shoes in _____ house.

   a you needn't, her

   b I needn't, our

   c I needn't, their

   d you needn't, our

9. Pradeep thought, "If I was younger, I would accept it."

Pradeep thought that if _____ was younger, _____ accept it.

   a I, I would

   b he, he would

   c I, he would

   d he, he will

10. Sudhir replied, "I have been watching a film."

Sudhir replied that _____ watching a film.

   a he has been

   b he was

   c he had been

   d I had been

Exercise II

Indirect to Direct

Select the correct option to complete the sentence given in direct speech in each question. In some questions there is more than one blank.

1. The Science teacher advised Lalita to work hard.
   The Science teacher said to Lalita, "______ hard."
   - a You work
   - b Work
   - c You can work
   - d You like to work

2. Mr Acharya asked the cook whether dinner was ready.
   Mr Acharya asked the cook, "______ ready?"
   - a Is dinner
   - b Will dinner be
   - c Dinner is
   - d Was dinner

3. The station master said that the Rajdhani Express train would stop there.
   The station master said, " The Rajdhani Express train ______."
   - a would stop here
   - b would stop there
   - c will stop here
   - d will stop there

4. Kapil said that there was no milk in the refrigerator.
   Kapil said, "______ milk in the refrigerator."
   - a There was no
   - b There is no
   - c Is there no
   - d There were no

5. Salim requested Krishna to help him do the homework.
   Salim told Krishna, "Please ______ the homework."
   - a do help me
   - b help do
   - c help me do
   - d helping me do

6. The police constable asked the thieves to halt immediately.
   The police constable said to the thieves, "______!"
   - a Halt immediately
   - b Immediately halt
   - c Stop now
   - d Now halt

7. Gunwant asked Dinesh whether he understood Bengali.
   Gunwant ____ Dinesh, "______ understand Bengali?"
   - a asked to, You do
   - b said to, You
   - c said, You do
   - d said to, Do you

8. Sarla said they had shifted to that house six months before.
   Sarla said, "We shifted to ______ house six months ______."
   - a this, before
   - b that, ago
   - c that, before
   - d this, ago

9. Ravi said that it had been raining all day.
   Ravi said, "It ______ all day."
   - a has been raining
   - b is raining
   - c had rained
   - d was raining

10. The minister said that they had tried to control the prices of vegetables the previous year.
    The minister said, "______ to control the prices of vegetables______ year."
    - a They tried, previous
    - b We try, last
    - c We tried, last
    - d They try, previous

Chapter 9

Punctuation and Spelling

Punctuation Marks

A Punctuation Mark is a mark such as a full stop, comma, question mark etc, used in writing to separate sentences and their parts and also to make the meaning clear. Capitalisation of letters is included under the topic of punctuation.

Sentence ending punctuation marks are period or full stop (.), question mark (?) and exclamation mark (!).

Examples
- The boy was awarded for his bravery.
- What are your hobbies?
- Wonderful! We won the match!

Breaks within sentences are denoted by *comma (,)*, *semi-colon (;)*, *colon (:)*, *hyphen (-)*, *dash (– or —)* and *parentheses* or *brackets* ((and)).

Examples
- The fruit basket contains apples, oranges and bananas.
- Das is going bald; his hair is getting thinner.
- My favourite movie is Lord of the Rings : The Two Towers.
- Preeti always like to be up-to-date.
- Pratiksha is the friend — the only friend — who offered me help.
- When he got home (it was already dark outside) he cooked dinner.

Other punctuation marks used are *double quotes* (" and "), *single quotes* (' and ') and *apostrophe* (').

Examples
- Mother asked me, "Do you want to eat anything?"
- Aman's marks are the highest in the class.

Spellings

Knowledge of spellings is essential to write any language. If there is a mistake in the spelling of the word, the meaning of the word may change. Hence one must have good knowledge of spellings of words.

The example given below is for better understanding of spellings.

Choose the correct spelling among the four options.

Example   Brijesh got ready for school and then ate his ______ (morning meal).

    a brakefast   b breekfast   c breakfust   d breakfast

Ans. (d) breakfast

Practice Centre

Exercise I
Using Commas

In each question, select the option with the correctly used commas.

1.
  a After Binod had washed his feet and hands he sat down to dinner.
  b After Binod had washed his feet, and hands, he sat down to dinner.
  c After Binod had washed his feet and hands, he sat down to dinner.
  d After Binod had, washed his feet, and hands, he sat down to dinner.

2.
  a The Kiwi, which is a bird, is native to New Zealand.
  b The Kiwi which is a bird, is native to New Zealand.
  c The Kiwi which is a bird is native to New Zealand.
  d The Kiwi, which is a bird is native to New Zealand.

3.
  a Mother, please don't allow Father to go, until I'm dressed.
  b Mother, please don't allow Father to go until I'm dressed.
  c Mother please don't allow Father to go until I'm dressed.
  d Mother please don't allow Father to go, until I'm dressed.

4.
  a My elder sister who will be eighteen soon is learning to drive a car.
  b My elder sister who will be eighteen soon, is learning to drive a car.
  c My elder sister, who will be eighteen soon is learning to drive a car.
  d My elder sister, who will be eighteen soon, is learning to drive a car.

5.
  a Cheese has more fat than butter, but I don't like cheese.
  b Cheese has more fat than butter but I don't like cheese.
  c Cheese has more fat, than butter, but I don't like cheese.
  d Cheese has more fat, than butter but I don't like cheese.

6.
  a As the sun was shining brightly it was very hot outside.
  b As the sun was shining brightly, it was very hot outside.
  c As the sun, was shining brightly, it was very hot outside.
  d As the sun, was shining brightly it was very hot outside.

7.
  a I wore my raincoat before going out, because I did not want to get wet in the rain.
  b I wore my raincoat before going out because I did not want to get wet in the rain.
  c I wore my raincoat, before going out, because I did not want to get wet in the rain.
  d I wore my raincoat, before going out, because I did not want to get wet, in the rain.

8.
  a Excuse me, sir, can you tell me the way to the railway station?
  b Excuse me sir can you tell me the way to the railway station?
  c Excuse me sir, can you tell me the way to the railway station?
  d Excuse me, sir, can you tell me the way, to the railway station?

9.
  a Dad will you leave me to the school or should I take the school bus?
  b Dad will you leave me to the school, or should I take the school bus?
  c Dad, will you leave me to the school or should I take the school bus?
  d Dad, will you leave me to the school, or should I take the school bus?

10.
  a As the principal entered the classroom, the students became silent.
  b As the principal entered the classroom the students became silent.
  c As the principal, entered the classroom, the students became silent.
  d As the principal entered, the classroom, the students, became silent.

Exercise II
Selection of Correctly Punctuated Sentences

In the questions given below, select the option which is correctly punctuated.

1. a My first job in an office was to write reports file papers and handle complaints.
   b My first job in an office was to write reports, file papers and handle complaints.
   c My first job in an office: was to write reports, file papers, and handle complaints
   d My first job in an office was to write reports, file papers, and handle complaints

2. a Mr Baretto has applied for the football coachs job this time but is not likely to be selected.
   b Mr Baretto has applied, for the football coachs job this time but is not likely to be selected.
   c Mr Baretto has applied for the football coach's job this time; but is not likely to be selected.
   d Mr Baretto has applied for the football coach's job this time, but is not likely to be selected.

3. a Sachin had decided to retire many years ago, but was persuaded not to do so.
   b Sachin had decided to retire many years ago but was persuaded not to do so.
   c Sachin had decided to retire many years ago; but was persuaded not to do so.
   d Sachin had decided to retire, many years ago but was persuaded not to do so.

4. a "Hey you, said Puneet, can you guide me to the bus stand?"
   b "Hey you" said Puneet "can you guide me to the bus stand".
   c "Hey you!" said Puneet, "Can you guide me to the bus stand?"
   d Hey you "said Puneet" can you guide me to the bus stand.

5. a Rahul are you too busy with games to even complete your homework?
   b Rahul, are you too busy with games to even complete your homework?
   c Rahul, are you too busy with games, to even complete your homework?
   d Rahul are you too busy with games to even complete your homework.

6. a Lata loves eating dosa, idli and sambar, Alok loves noodles chicken soup and sweet sour vegetables.
   b Lata loves eating dosa, idli and sambar Alok loves noodles, chicken, soup and sweet, sour vegetables.
   c Lata loves eating dosa, idli and sambar; Alok loves noodles, tomato soup and sweet sour vegetables.
   d Lata loves eating dosa idli and sambar; Alok loves noodles chicken soup and sweet sour vegetables.

7. a Isnt it shameful that a sincere politician like Rakesh, is not getting elected?
   b Isnt it shameful that a sincere politician like Rakesh is not getting elected.
   c Isn't it shameful that a sincere politician like Rakesh, is not getting elected?
   d Isn't it shameful that a sincere politician like Rakesh is not getting elected?

8. a My favourite teacher, who also happens to be my uncle, retired recently.
   b My favourite teacher; who also happens to be my uncle; retired recently.
   c My favourite teacher, who also happens to be my uncle; retired recently.
   d My favourite teacher who also happens to be my uncle retired recently.

9. a Three major cities, Mumbai, Chennai, and Kolkata, had the first universities in India.
   b Three major cities Mumbai, Chennai and Kolkata, had the first universities in India.
   c Three major cities – Mumbai, Chennai and Kolkata - had the first universities in India.
   d Three major cities, Mumbai Chennai and Kolkata, had the first universities in India.

10. a Your concerns this year, however should be staying healthy finding a job and getting married.
    b Your concerns this year, however, should be staying healthy, finding a job and getting married.
    c Your concerns this year, however, should be staying healthy, finding a job, and getting married.
    d Your concerns this year however should be staying healthy finding a job and getting married.

Exercise III

Multiple Choice Quiz on Punctuation

Fill in the blanks in the sentences given below with the correct punctuation mark by selecting from the options given. The different punctuation marks in each option are separated by '/'. The option '(none)' means that no punctuation mark is to be put.

1. Jagdish is tired___ He___s going home___
   a colon / comma / period
   b semi-colon / (none) / period
   c period / apostrophe / period
   d colon / apostrophe / period

2. ___Cheer up mother___ I___ll get work somewhere___ ___
   a (none) / comma / apostrophe / period / (none)
   b double quotes / comma / apostrophe / period / double quotes
   c (none) / (none) / apostrophe / period / (none)
   d double quotes / comma / (none) / period / double quotes

3. Karun ___ s father said to him ___ ___ Please stay at home as it is raining hard___ ___
   a (none) / comma / double quotes / question mark / double quotes
   b apostrophe / comma / (none) / period / (none)
   c apostrophe / comma / (none) / period / (none)
   d apostrophe / comma / double quotes / period / double quotes

4. Four magazines that I regularly read are___ Science Today___ Sarita___ Chandamama and Filmfare___
   a semi - colon / comma / comma / period
   b colon / (none) / (none) / period
   c period / comma / comma / period
   d colon / comma / comma / period

5. She asked___ ___What is the title of your new novel___ ___
   a colon / double quotes / question mark / double quotes
   b comma / double quotes / period / double quotes
   c comma / double quotes / question mark / double quotes
   d question mark / (none) / period / (none)

6. Please arrive on time ___ All late arrivals ___ will have to wait until intermission to enter ___
   a colon / comma / period
   b period / (none) / period
   c exclamation mark / comma / period
   d question mark / (none) / period

7. The instructor walks into class ___ takes attendance ___ asks for homework ___ and begins class ___
   a colon / comma / comma / period
   b period / (none) / comma / period
   c comma / comma / (none) / period
   d question mark / (none) / comma / period

8. His father exclaimed___ ___Alas___ My son___ you have missed the train___ ___
   a colon / (none) / comma / exclamation mark / period / (none)
   b comma / double quotes / exclamation mark / comma / period / double quotes
   c exclamation mark / (none) / comma / period / period / (none)
   d question mark / double quotes / (none) / comma / period / double quotes

9. The traveller asked me the way to a nearby hotel___as he wanted to stay there___
   a comma / period
   b (none) / period
   c colon / period
   d semi-colon / period

10. Slice an apple in half ___ and sprinkle 1 tsp or 5 ml of cinnamon on top ___ Place the two halves on a sheet of foil ___ place in the oven ___ and bake ___
    a (none) / period / comma / (none) / period
    b period / (none) / comma / comma / period
    c semi-colon / comma / comma / (none) / period
    d question mark / (none) / period / comma / period

Exercise IV

Spelling Words Related to Professions and Occupations

Complete the blanks with the name of the profession described in brackets with its correct spelling from the options given.

1. Neil Armstrong was the first ______ (space traveller) to step on the moon.
   - a astronaut
   - b asteronaut
   - c astronot
   - d aestronaut

2. The forest fire was put out with difficulty by the ______. (those who put out fires)
   - a farman
   - b fairmen
   - c firmen
   - d firemen

3. All the furniture in Shakeel's office was made by a wonderful ______ (wood worker) named Ali.
   - a caurpunter
   - b caprenter
   - c carpenter
   - d carpentar

4. The ______ (nurse for chilbirth) delivered Malti's second baby very carefully.
   - a maidwife
   - b mildwife
   - c midwife
   - d midwif

5. Kapil's elder sister is the ______ (typing letters, keeping recods) of a manager in a big company.
   - a sectry
   - b secretary
   - c secretery
   - d sacratary

6. The traffic ______ (upholder of the law) fined my father ₹ 100 for driving through a red light.
   - a poliseman
   - b puliceman
   - c policman
   - d policeman

7. Ashok's father works as an ______ (working with electricity).
   - a electrician
   - b electrican
   - c lectician
   - d electrical

8. Ravi quarelled with a ______ (serving food) in the restaurant because there was a delay in serving him food.
   - a vaiter
   - b waitar
   - c weiter
   - d waiter

9. The ______ (player of music) played the harmonium very badly.
   - a musican
   - b musician
   - c musical
   - d myusician

10. Mr Kala is our Science ______ (staff of school).
    - a tichher
    - b ticher
    - c teacher
    - d teecher

Exercise V

Spelling Words Related to Travelling

Complete the blanks with words related to travelling described in brackets with their correct spelling from the options given.

1. Our picnic party went on a wonderful ride on a ______ (boat with engine) in Mumbai harbour.
   - a motrboat
   - b motorboat
   - c motorbot
   - d motarboat

2. My uncle's ______ (bank card) was able to help us when we did not have money to buy gifts.
   - a credit card
   - b cradit card
   - c credet card
   - d kredit card

3. My sister's ______ (item of luggage) was already full, so she gave some of her clothes to put in mine.
   - a suitcaise
   - b sutcase
   - c suitcase
   - d sootcase

4. The ______ (running on rails) trains in Europe are very luxurious.
   - a railwey
   - b raleway
   - c ralway
   - d railway

5. The ______ (porter) found it easy to carry my light luggage to platform no 16.
   - a coolie
   - b culie
   - c kuli
   - d kooli

6. The ______ (document showing roads) issued by the agency was very helpful.
   - a rod map
   - b road map
   - c road mep
   - d rood map

7. The _______ (female cabin crew in aircraft) announced that we should fasten our seat belts, as we were going to take off soon.

   a air hastess   b air hustes

   c air hostas   d air hostess

8. The _______ (leaflet giving details) of the Shikhar Hotel was very impressive.

   a brochar   b brosure

   c brochure   d broshure

9. Jiwan took so many photos of the wonderful _______ (view) that his digital camera ran out of memory.

   a scenry   b scenery

   c senary   d seenery

10. Manju's _______ (document needed for travel abroad) arrived just in time for her trip to Dubai.

   a paaspurt   b paasport

   c pasport   d passport

Exercise VI

Correcting the Spelling of Misspelled Words in a Story

In the story given below, select the correct spellings of the words spelt wrongly (marked by numbers just after them) from the options given.

Mysterious Noises

There is a very strange sound comeing **1.** from the attic. It could be a mouse, but I sure hope its not! I just rememberd **2.** that our neighbour warned us about bats. My brother thinks I'm only imaging **3.** the noises. Our little sister is so afriad **4.** that she's crying. I'm trying to forget about it, but the mysteryous **5.** sounds continue. I'd love to ask Mother what could be causeing **6.** the rattling. I cann't **7.** find her anywhere in the house or the backyard. Bravly **8.** I make the decision to see what is the matter by myself. Quitely **9.** and cautiously, I climb the ladder into the attic. When I finaly **10.** reach the top, I start laughing uncontrolably **11.** There's Mother, moving boxes of our old cloths **12.** and toys!

Options

1.   a calming   b cooming

     c comeeng   d coming

2.   a remembered   b rembered

     c remainbered   d rimembered

3.   a magining   b imagining

     c imagineing   d imegining

4.   a aifrid   b afeard

     c afraid   d afaraid

5.   a mysteries   b mysterys

     c mysterious   d misterious

6.   a cusing   b causing

     c cosing   d causinge

7.   a canno't   b cant

     c can't   d kan't

8.   a Braively   b Braveley

     c Bereavely   d Bravely

9.   a Quiettly   b Quietly

     c Quitly   d Quitley

10.   a fainally   b finnally

     c finally   d finilly

11.   a uncantrollable   b uncantrolably

     c uncuntrollably   d uncontrollably

12.   a clothes   b cloth

     c clouths   d klothes

Chapter 10

Sentence Rearrangement

Sentence rearrangement refers to arranging the parts of a sentence in a logical manner or rearranging sentences of a paragraph in logical order.

Sentence Rearrangement is of two types :

Type A Rearranging the parts of a sentence to form a meaningful sentence.

Example
        all kings wisest of was the Solomon.
          P   Q   R   S

    a PRQS   **b** SRQP   **c** PRSQ   **d** QPSR

Ans. (b)

Type B Rearranging sentences to form a meaningful paragraph.

Example
    P : By doing so, Kolkata will be the first in South Asia.
    Q : They run down the centre of the road.
    R : Kolkata, unlike other cities, kept its trams.
    S : To ease the traffic on the road, government decided to build underground railway lines.

    a RQSP   **b** SRQP   **c** PQSR   **d** QPSR

Ans. (a)

Practice Centre

Exercise I

Type A

The parts of each sentence have been jumbled up and are marked as P, Q, R and S. Rearrange the parts to form the sentence correctly and select the correct option accordingly.

1. my mouth tasty dishes make these water.
      P   Q   R S
    a PSRQ   **b** RQSP   **c** PQSR   **d** RQPS

2. early indications often there are of the coming changes.
        P   Q   R   S
    a QRSP   **b** PRQS   **c** QRPS   **d** SRQP

3. greatest monarchs Chandragupta was of India one of the.
           P   Q   R   S

   a QSPR   b QRSP   c SPRQ   d SQRP

4. very grateful for his kindness to him they were.
           P   Q   R   S

   a PSRQ   b SPRQ   c PQSR   d SPQR

5. with a huge lion had to fight kept in a cage the slave.
           P   Q   R   S

   a RSQP   b RSPQ   c SQPR   d SRPQ

6. of a river was cutting a tree on the bank one day a poor woodcutter.
           P   Q   R   S

   a SRQP   b RPQS   c RSPQ   d SQRP

7. taken against accidents, are injured in spite of the precautions many people in factories.
           P   Q   R   S

   a SQPR   b RPSQ   c QPRS   d RPQS

8. in verse the stories are selected and are written from epics and mythologies.
           P   Q   R   S

   a QSRP   b QPRS   c PSRQ   d SRQP

9. preserve and destroy deities who create, mythology, there are three according to Indian.
           P   Q   R   S

   a SQRP   b RQPS   c SRQP   d PRQS

10. is to use the words the only really effective way in reading and writing of learning how to spell correctly.
           P   Q   R   S

   a QPSR   b RQSP   c SRQP   d QSPR

Exercise II

Type B

In each question, arrange the four sentences given in each question labelled as P,Q, R and S to form a logical paragraph and accordingly select the correct option.

1. P : We all use money in our lives.

   Q : We use coins and notes as well as credit cards.

   R : We think that coins were first used in China and then in ancient Greece.

   S : In olden days people used shells, beans, salt and even animals.

     a QSRP   b SRQP

     c PQSR   d QPSR

2. P : Thus, they are a good advertisement for vegetarianism.

   Q : The African elephants are larger with longer tusks and bigger ears.

   R : Elephants live entirely on leaves, grass and roots.

   S : Elephants are found in India and Africa.

     a SRQP   b RPQS

     c RSPQ   d SQRP

3. P : As the vapour rises, it cools.

   Q : The droplets come together and form a cloud.

   R : The sun evaporates water from lakes and oceans.

   S : The water vapour condenses into tiny droplets of water.

     a SQPR   b RPSQ

     c QPRS   d RPQS

4. P : However, some elderly people find it difficult to use it.

   Q : Twenty years ago school children had not heard of the internet.

   R : In fact many of us use it even from our homes.

   S : Now there is nobody who has not heard of it.

     a QSRP   b QPRS

     c PSRQ   d SRQP

5. P : Another example of an unlucky omen is a black cat crossing your path.

Q : For instance, do you believe that if you walk under a ladder, you will have bad luck for the rest of the day?

R : Are you superstitious?

S : However, I do not believe in these things, as I am not superstitious.

a	SQRP	b	RQPS
c	SRQP	d	PRQS

6. P : These precautions will help in preventing such diseases.

Q : However, everyone can take precautions to stop the mosquitoes from breeding.

R : In some poor parts of the world, people die from these diseases because they are not able to buy the required medicines.

S : Mosquitoes are pests that can cause diseases such as malaria and dengue.

a	QPSR	b	RQSP
c	SRQP	d	QSPR

7. P : They must also be trained properly, as they have to use complicated equipment like fire hoses and breathing apparatus.

Q : Lastly, they have to be courageous because sometimes they need to enter burning buildings to rescue people.

R : They have to be fit and strong because sometimes they have to climb tall ladders to bring people out of burning buildings.

S : Fire fighters have to be very fit, well trained and brave.

a	RSQP	b	RSPQ
c	SRQP	d	SRPQ

8. P : It was about the polar ice caps.

Q : Apparently, with global warming, the ice near the poles is beginning to melt.

R : The programme showed the result – mountains of ice were breaking off and falling into the sea.

S : Last night I watched an interesting programme on the National Geographic Channel on TV.

a	PSRQ	b	SPRQ
c	PQSR	d	SPQR

9. P : There is something magical about actually seeing and touching snow.

Q : Of course, I had seen pictures of snow, but had never seen the real thing.

R : I live in Africa and I have never actually seen snow.

S : Then one day I got the chance to go to Canada, where my uncle stays.

a	QRSP	b	PRQS
c	QRPS	d	SRQP

10. P : Do you know why?

Q : Once there was a boy named Kamlesh who did not have any friends.

R : It was because he was short tempered and used to argue on every matter.

S : His parents were not happy with him and his teachers also did not like him.

a	QSPR	b	QRSP
c	SPRQ	d	SQRP

Chapter 11

Synonyms and Antonyms

Synonyms

A synonym of a word is a word or expression that has the same meaning as the original word.
e.g. Happy – Glad

Antonyms

An antonym of a word is a word or expression that has a meaning opposite to that of the original word. e.g. Happy – Sad

Practice Centre

Exercise I
Finding Synonyms

In each of the following questions, select the option which is a synonym of the word given.

1. Appear
| a arise | b close | c end | d open |

2. Hunt
| a find | b explore | c search | d check |

3. Error
| a misprint | b misbehaviour | c accident | d mistake |

4. Average
| a special | b ordinary | c cheap | d boring |

5. Fool
| a simple | b difficult | c idiot | d pretending |

6. Reply
| a announce | b speak | c describe | d respond |

7. Daybreak
| a morning | b breakfast | c forenoon | d sunlight |

8. Unattractive
| a Beautiful | b Ugly | c Plain | d novelty |

9. Periodically
| a newspaper | b magazine | c regularly | d monthly |

10. Middle
| a diagonal | b circle | c inside | d centre |

Exercise II

Finding Synonyms in Context

In each of the following questions, select the option which is a synonym of the word underlined in the sentence given.

1. It was a house having very <u>few</u> comforts.
   - a Little
   - b Poor
   - c Insufficient
   - d Abundant

2. Sujata <u>learnt</u> swimming before she was six years old.
   - a Discovered
   - b Educated
   - c Started
   - d Mastered

3. Unless you do as I tell you, everybody will <u>surely</u> die.
   - a Firmly
   - b Certainly
   - c Confidently
   - d Unlikely

4. Kavita can go home because she has <u>finished</u> her test.
   - a Accomplished
   - b Ended
   - c Expert
   - d Completed

5. Salim likes chocolates but his brother Javed does not like <u>sweet</u> things.
   - a Pleasant
   - b Sugary
   - c Tasty
   - d Delicious

6. Search his pockets and you will <u>find</u> my stolen mobile phone in one of them.
   - a Reach
   - b Encounter
   - c Retrieve
   - d Pinpoint

7. Rahul will get hurt if he is not <u>careful</u>.
   - a Watchful
   - b Diligent
   - c Thoughtful
   - d Frugal

8. Because the monsoon rains were poor this year, there is <u>scarcity</u> of foodgrains in the country.
   - a Less
   - b Reduce
   - c Shortage
   - d Abundance

9. We must bathe daily to <u>remain</u> in good health.
   - a Survive
   - b Wait
   - c Balance
   - d Continue

10. You must wash all vegetables <u>thoroughly</u> before cooking them.
    - a Utterly
    - b Sincerely
    - c Rigorously
    - d Sparingly

Exercise III

Finding Antonyms

In each of the following questions, select the option which is an antonym of the word given.

1. Laudable
   - a Courageous
   - b Coward
   - c Shameful
   - d Admirable

2. Relinquish
   - a Join
   - b Give
   - c Leave
   - d Retain

3. Economical
   - a Miserly
   - b Extravagant
   - c Rich
   - d Poor

4. Prohibit
   - a Refuse
   - b Licence
   - c Allow
   - d Tolerate

5. Genuine
   - a False
   - b Variable
   - c Foolish
   - d Unreliable

6. Hopeful
   - a Unsure
   - b Unhappy
   - c Pitiable
   - d Despairing

7. Virtuous
   - a Shocking
   - b Wicked
   - c Mischievous
   - d Excellent

8. Fickle
   - a Faithful
   - b Constant
   - c Useful
   - d Undependable

9. Adverse
   - a Similar
   - b Profitable
   - c Injurious
   - d Favourable

10. Sagacious
    - a Expert
    - b Knowledgeable
    - c Unwise
    - d Useless

Exercise IV

Finding Antonyms in Context

In each of the following questions, select the option which is an antonym of the word underlined in the sentence given.

1. The strain of it all was getting to us, and the boredom was becoming unbearable.
   - a Stress
   - b Struggle
   - c Relief
   - d Relaxed

2. How did the crew members make certain that they had found the correct ship?
   - a Careless
   - b Uncheck
   - c Right
   - d Wrong

3. Their small island was an equatorial paradise with lush green forests and waters full of fish.
   - a Hot
   - b Polar
   - c Temperate
   - d Marine

4. Boiling enhances the flavour as well as adding colour to the sap.
   - a Diminishes
   - b Increases
   - c Clears
   - d Concentrates

5. Instead of drinking water, frogs absorb it through the thin skin on their abdomen.
   - a Swallow
   - b Use
   - c Emit
   - d Exit

6. The sugar maple tree is used for making furniture, interior woodwork, flooring and crates.
   - a Forming
   - b Dismantling
   - c Creation
   - d Destroying

Exercise V

Finding Synonyms and Antonyms of Words in a Passage

In the passage given below, some words have been underlined. You have to find synonyms or antonyms of these words, depending on what is mentioned in brackets just after the underlined word. To help you, four options are given for each answer below the passage.

Flying Frogs of Borneo

In hang gliding, the pilot jumps off a cliff or hilltop and sails through the air at a gradual downward slant, held aloft (1) (*antonym*) by lightweight "wings" strapped to a harness. The pilot controls the craft by shifting his or her weight, or by changing (2) (*antonym*) the angle of the wings.

Flying frogs do much the same thing. With powerful hind (3) (*antonym*) legs they launch their lightweight bodies from a high branch into the air. They spread (4) (*antonym*) out their large webbed feet and hands, as well as special flaps of skin on their legs and arms. These membranes (5) (*synonym*) of skin act like miniature parachutes to slow the frog's descent.

Some flying frogs glide (6) (*synonym*) as far as 40 or 50 feet as they descend by stages (7) (*synonym*) from the treetops to vegetation lower down. For these little animals, gliding is an energy efficient (8) (*synonym*) way to get quickly from one place to another. By moving its legs or twisting (9) (*synonym*) its toes, the flying frog can even turn as it glides, so it can land to the right or left of its original (10) (*antonym*) direction of launch.

1.	a below	b under	c above	d behind
2.	a steadying	b developing	c altering	d fixing
3.	a back	b rear	c fore	d front
4.	a suppress	b fold	c extend	d scatter
5.	a flaps	b husks	c coverings	d skins
6.	a soar	b fly	c drift	d slip
7.	a parts	b theatres	c phases	d groups
8.	a organised	b competent	c perfect	d proficient
9.	a crumpling	b wriggling	c winding	d turning
10.	a false	b authentic	c final	d ending

Chapter 12

Idioms and Phrases

Idioms

An idiom is an expression of a given language that is peculiar to itself grammatically. It cannot be understood if we take the meanings of the individual words used in the idiom.

Example
To Bell the cat (to take first step at one's own risk) — Everyone wanted to complain, but no one was ready *to bell the cat*.

Phrases

A phrase is a sequence of words that have meaning especially when forming part of a sentence.

Example
Look after (to take care) — My parents *look after* us patiently.

Practice Centre

Exercise I
Identifying Meanings of Idioms and Phrases

Identify the meanings of the idioms given by selecting the correct option, as given in the example.

1. Rings a bell
   a Alarms you
   b Very noisy
   c Disturbing news
   d Is familiar, but can't remember where it was heard

2. Get wind of
   a Find out   b Hear from somebody   c Feel a gentle breeze   d Step out in a storm

3. Easy as pie
   a Making pies is very easy   b Anybody can make pies
   c Very simple   d Foolish person

4. Burn the candle at both ends
   a Light a candle both in the night and the day   b Use the candle till the very end
   c Run very fast   d Work long hours

5. Chicken out
   a Forget to do something
   b A chicken which has run away
   c Avoid doing something because of fear
   d Catching a chicken which has run away

6. Too many cooks spoil the broth
   a If too many people cook broth, it will be spoiled.
   b If too many people get involved in a work, it will not be done properly.
   c The best work is done by a single person.
   d Only one person should cook broth.

7. Going by the book
   a Reading carefully
   b Following a book
   c Reading a book
   d Following the rules

8. The lion's share
   a A fair share
   b The largest amount
   c The deserved share
   d The least amount

9. White elephant
   a Something much more expensive than its value
   b Something very rare
   c An elephant which has lost its colour
   d A thing which has never been heard of before

10. Have your cake and eat it too
   a Eat more than your share
   b Get two cakes instead of one
   c Have the advantage of both alternatives
   d Enjoy the food

Exercise II
Correct Meanings of Idioms and Phrases

Identify the meanings of the idioms given by selecting the correct option.

1. To end in smoke
   a Religious ceremony
   b Face failure
   c House burnt down
   d Smoking too many cigarettes

2. To get into hot water
   a Bathe in the winter months
   b To get healthy
   c To get rich
   d To get into trouble

3. Bolt from the blue
   a Sudden shock
   b Get punched
   c Lose a tight game
   d Ask for help

4. Bury the hatchet
   a Kill someone
   b Overexert
   c End enmity
   d Hide stolen treasure

5. Spill the beans
   a Eat clumsily   b Reveal a secret
   c Get exhausted   d Fight carelessly

6. Lead up the garden path
   a Give directions
   b Show a beautiful place
   c Mislead
   d Exaggerate

7. Weather a storm
   a Guess correctly
   b Criticise someone
   c Become an introvert
   d Survive a crisis

8. Give a hand
   a Help
   b Use the hand
   c Hand out
   d Share something

9. Give it a shot
   a Shoot it   b Try
   c Use a gun   d Help

10. Bite your lip
   a Use your teeth
   b Become violent
   c Not react despite being angry
   d React strongly

Exercise III

Understanding Idioms and Phrases in Context

In the following questions, the idiom / phrase is underlined. Identify its meaning by selecting the correct option.

1. Rajesh had to <u>pay through his nose</u> to buy the new smartphone.
   a pay the correct price
   b pay by holding your breath
   c pay a very high price
   d pay while breathing hard

2. Sameer has done his part of this project - now <u>the ball is in my court</u>.
   a I have to solve the problem
   b it is my turn to hit the ball
   c I must play it
   d it's my responsibility to work on it

3. Kavita did not believe what she heard; instead, she <u>read between the lines</u>.
   a inferred the real meaning of what is written or said.
   b understood what had not been said
   c read the small print between the lines
   d asked somebody else to explain what has been said

4. The authorities are going to <u>tear down</u> that building because it is built illegally.
   a cut
   b dismantle or demolish
   c rip apart
   d remove

5. As Basit broke the window of the house adjoining the park, he will have to <u>face the music</u>.
   a listen to what music the house owner plays
   b run away for some time
   c look at the house owner playing music
   d accept the unpleasant result of his action

6. To succeed in running a cinema hall business, you have to <u>keep your eyes on the ball</u>.
   a watch the ball carefully
   b earn a good profit
   c remain alert to what is occurring around you
   d keep the prices of tickets low

7. William has <u>changed his tune</u> since Jamshed was promoted ahead of him.
   a worn a different dress
   b changed his manner of working
   c started playing a different tune on the piano
   d been keeping quiet

8. Harsh <u>backed down from supporting</u> the plan when he saw that all others were against it.
   a reduced his support for
   b stepped down from his support
   c took back his support for
   d increased his support for

9. Sarla's position is bad now, and if she leaves her job, she'll go <u>from the frying pan into the fire</u>.
   a from a bad situation to a worse situation
   b will not use the frying pan for cooking
   c he will not earn anything
   d get burned badly

10. Raman is the <u>black sheep</u> of the family because he is often jailed for burglaries.
    a having the darkest coloured skin
    b owning a black coloured sheep
    c best person
    d person who causes shame or embarrassment

Exercise IV
Story with Idioms

In the story given below, identify the meanings of the idioms and phrases underlined by selecting from the options given below.

A Horror Story

One evening, Kapil is driving from the city where he works to his village and decides to take the old road, not the highway, to enjoy the scenery. When he reaches the hills, his car breaks down. **1.** As the nearest town is too far away to reach on foot **2.** he tries to get a lift from any passing car. Soon he sees a big red car coming towards him. Its driver is burning rubber **3.** and does not stop. All at once **4.** the clouds darken and it starts raining cats and dogs. **5.** As darkness falls and it is still raining, an old blue car comes slowly down the road. It stops next to him. He opens the back door, jumps in, and leans forward to thank his saviour – but there is no one at the wheel!

Although the car is driverless and its engine is not running, it starts to move again. Kapil is scared out of his wits **6.** but looks at the road ahead and sees a bend in the road. Just before the car reaches there, a hairy hand appears through the window and turns the steering wheel so that the car easily turns and remains on the road.

Looking as pale as death **7.** Kapil watches as the hand appears several times to prevent the car from plunging down the hill. Then Kapil sees a blaze of bright lights a short distance away. Heart racing, he wrenches the door open, scrambles out, and runs for dear life **8.** towards the lights, thinking that he has reached a town. He is out of breath **9.** when he stumbles into a coffee shop, where he orders a cup of coffee to ease his nervousness. After finishing it, he starts telling his story to the coffee shop owner.

As he is telling his story, two bulky men wearing leather jackets and peaked caps come into the coffee shop. The taller one says to the shorter one, "See that man over there whose clothes are all wet? I'm going to knock the stuffing out of **10.** him!"

"Why? What did he do?"

With fury in his eyes, the big man says, "That's the idiot who got into our car while we were pushing it!"

1.   a Stops running
    b Separates into constituent parts
    c Is demolished or destroyed
    d Becomes distressed
	6. a Not scared b Gone mad
	    c Be very witty d Terrified

2.   a Wearing shoes
    b On your toes
    c Easily
    d Walking, instead travelling in a car
	7. a Having no blood
	    b Murdered
	    c Pale in the face due to fear
	    d Like a coward

3.   a Burning tyres   b Driving very fast
    c Lighting a fire   d Using matches
	8. a Desperately b Smartly
	    c Easily d Slowly and carefully

4.   a Together   b Jointly
    c Suddenly   d With each other
	9. a Not breathing
	    b Breathing easily
	    c Whispering
	    d Breathing with difficulty

5.   a Raining animals
    b Raining heavily
    c Cats fighting with dogs
    d Animals falling from the sky
	10. a Praise
	    b Make him vomit
	    c Give a severe beating to
	    d Kill

Chapter 13

Analogy

Analogy means a comparison based on similarity between like features of two things. It can also refer to the relation between the target word and the source word. Thus, the target word shares a necessary and direct relationship with the source word.

Such analogies are also expressed as "P is to Q as R is to S." or in the symbolic form of P : Q : : R : S.

Example

Entrepreneur : Profit : : Scholar : ?

    a Income   b Knowledge   c Service   d Business

  Ans. (b) As Entrepreneur wants Profit, Scholar wants Knowledge.

Practice Centre

Exercise I

P : Q is given and you have to find the correct R : S from the four options given.

1. Work : Earn
    a Influence : Assist   b Expect : Think   c Tender : Lovable   d Plant : Harvest

2. Aeroplane : Flying
    a Aeroplane : Airport   b Sailboat : Harbour   c Ship : Sailing   d Glider : Park

3. Heat : cooked
    a Cold : Frozen   b Ice : Skating   c Cold : Ice cream   d Chilly : Thaw

4. Claw : Cat
    a Cat : Whiskers   b Wag : Tail   c Tail : Dog   d Tooth : Bite

5. Pencil : Write
    a Knife : Grind   b Spoon : Stir   c Fork : Cut   d Pen : Ink

6. Fish : Fin
    a Bird : Wing   b Eagle : Beak   c Bird : Feather   d Fish : Water

7. Funny : Laughter
    a Humorous : Yawning   b Sleep : Dreaming   c Sadness : Hunger   d Sorrow : Crying

8. Ballerina : Dancing
    a Ballet : Dancer   b Vocalist : Singing   c Actor : Music   d Driver : Accident

9. Loud : Scream
    a Valley : Forest   b Shout : Talk   c Yell : Talk   d Quiet : Whisper

10. Shoe : Foot
    a Mitten : Arm   b Glove : Hand   c Glove : Finger   d Nostril : Nose

Exercise II

Three words/phrases out of P, Q, R and S are given and you have to find the correct ? from the four options given.

1. Wet : Dry up : : Hot : ?
   a Heat up
   b Cool down
   c Dry off
   d Freeze

2. Spoke : Wheel : : Wheel : ?
   a Transportation
   b Ride
   c Pavement
   d Bicycle

3. Clock : Time : : Thermometer : ?
   a Temperature
   b Fever
   c Illness
   d Heat

4. Weighing scale : Weight : : Ruler : ?
   a Weigh
   b Measure
   c Length
   d Long

5. Leaf : Tree : : ? : Flower
   a Stem
   b Garden
   c Bush
   d Petal

6. Leave : ? : : Get up : Go to sleep
   a Eat
   b Arrive
   c Drive
   d Bathe

7. Judge : Court : : Policeman : ?
   a Parliament
   b The Police force
   c Police Station
   d Army

8. City : State : : ? : Country
   a State
   b Continent
   c Land
   d Sea

9. Family : Child : : ? : Student
   a Class
   b Teacher
   c Parents
   d Sister

10. Corn : Cob : : ? : Pod
   a Green
   b Pea
   c Can
   d Beans

Exercise III

Find the option which is different from the others in any way from the other options given. This means that one of the four options given does not belong to the group of the other three.

1. a Donkey   b Cat
        c Dragon   d Dog

2. a Banana   b Apple
        c Peach   d Tomato

3. a Cell phone   b Laptop
        c Electronic camera d Street light

4. a Airliner   b Truck
        c Bus   d Express Train

5. a Hatred   b Anger
        c Love   d Fear

6. a Hotel   b Inn
        c House   d Classroom

7. a Bottle   b Water
        c Pencil   d Shop

8. a Tree branch   b Iceberg
        c Boat   d Hammer

9. a Window   b Wall
        c Table   d Floor

10. a Coat   b Scarf
        c Gloves   d Shorts

Cloze Test

Cloze tests require the ability to understand context and vocabulary in order to identify the correct words or type of words that belong to the missing parts of a text. A Cloze Test is a procedure in which we are asked to supply words that have been removed from a passage as a test of our ability to understand the given text.

Practice Centre

Exercise I
Grammar Cloze

Fill in each blank with the most suitable word from the options given below the passage.

Girish was walking to his class quickly, as he was late. He was worried **1.** ______ the Environment Science test he **2.** ______ have to take **3.** ______ morning. As he was reaching the stairs **4.** ______ going up **5.** ______ the classroom, a piece of paper suddenly fluttered down and landed near his feet. As Girish glanced down **6.** ______ the paper, his heart nearly missed a beat. It was the Environment Science test paper complete **7.** ______ answers!

Girish's very first thought was not to tell anyone about **8.** ______ he had found. He **9.** ______ memorise all the answers and do extremely well **10.** ______ the test. After some hard thinking, however, he knew that it **11.** ______ be a dishonest thing to do. **12.** ______, it would not be fair **13.** ______ his classmates. In the end, Girish returned the paper **14.** ______ his Environment Science teacher, Mr Kala.

"Thanks, Girish. I have been searching high and low for it", said the teacher.

"I...I've read all the questions already, Sir", Girish confessed.

Mr Kala told him not to worry as he **15.** ______ think of new questions for the test. Girish's heart sank. He was half hoping that the test **16.** ______ be cancelled. Nevertheless, he did his best in the new test later that day. Three days later, the answer papers were returned to the class. To his pleasant surprise, Girish discovered **17.** ______ he had scored 80% marks. "You know something", he told his friends, "I **18.** ______ easily have scored full marks if I had cheated on **19.** ______ test. But I **20.** ______ be as pleased as I am now with the 80% marks I obtained."

1.	a in	b at	**4.**	a to	b on
	c about	d for		c for	d at
2.	a could	b can	**5.**	a at	b to
	c need	d would		c which	d this
3.	a same	b that	**6.**	a at	b for
	c these	d those		c what	d of

7.	a in	b with		**14.**	a for	b of
	c for	d at			c in	d to
8.	a that	b those		**15.**	a would	b try
	c what	d these			c may	d cannot
9.	a need	b would		**16.**	a should	b would
	c shall	d will			c was	d be
10.	a for	b of		**17.**	a this	b these
	c at	d in			c those	d that
11.	a should	b would		**18.**	a couldn't	b won't
	c wouldn't	d couldn't			c could	d will
12.	a Besides	b Sure		**19.**	a those	b this
	c Definite	d Yes			c these	d another
13.	a for	b at		**20.**	a will	b can't
	c to	d in			c hope	d wouldn't

Exercise II
Vocabulary Cloze

Complete the story using the most suitable words from the options given below the passage.

Last Saturday morning, a bank **1.** ________ went to a bank in Sector 11, NOIDA. He gave the bank cashier a canvas bag, pointed a **2.** ______ at her and said, "Give me the **3.** _____! Hurry!"

The cashier put the money in the bag, but when the robber turned to leave, the cashier pressed a silent alarm button with her **4.** ______. The alarm alerted the police.

When the police arrived at the bank, the robber was in the lobby. He was pointing his gun at the bank branch **5.** _____ and his assistant. They both had their hands up in the air. The police **6.** _____ the bank and blocked the front door and the back door. They trapped the robber inside the bank.

The police Inspector used a megaphone and told the robber to put down his gun and come out with his hands up in the **7.** ______. The bank robber said no. He said he would never **8.** _____. While the Inspector talked to the robber, two **9.** _____ entered the bank from a secret **10.** _______. They arrested the bank robber.

1.	a killer	b worker		**6.**	a surrounded	b exited
	c robber	d captain			c shouted	d opened
2.	a bomb	b gun		**7.**	a water	b head
	c cannon	d spoon			c air	d atmosphere
3.	a passbook	b jewels		**8.**	a think	b surrender
	c sweets	d cash			c do	d attack
4.	a head	b keys		**9.**	a children	b passengers
	c neck	d foot			c robbers	d policemen
5.	a peon	b manager		**10.**	a door	b chair
	c furniture	d guests			c roof	d bed

Exercise III
Comprehension Cloze

Fill in each blank with the most suitable word from the options given below the passage.

Karunesh and Mohnish are brothers. They moved from **1.** _______ to the United Kingdom in 1997. Karunesh speaks more English than Mohnish because he took English classes for two **2.** _____.

"Why do you always watch TV shows in English?" asks Mohnish. "You know I don't **3.** _______ them very well." "It helps me improve my English", says Karunesh. "Besides, I like English TV **4.** _____."

"I don't like them", says Mohnish. "I don't understand what the people are saying. They speak too **5.** _______." "That's because you didn't take English classes. I told you to come to class with **6.** _____", says Karunesh.

"I speak English pretty well. That's why I'm talking to you in English", says Mohnish. "I don't need classes."

"If you speak English so well, why can't you understand the people on TV?" **7.** ____ Karunesh.

"Because they speak **8.** _____ fast. I already told you that. Don't you listen?" says Mohnish.

"I heard you. Your English is pretty good, but it would be better if you took classes", says Karunesh. "The **9.** _____ I went to also has job training classes. You should go."

"I'll think about it", **10.** _______ Mohnish.

1.	a home	b nowhere		**6.**	a ours	b I
	c London	d India			c you	d me
2.	a days	b students		**7.**	a says	b asks
	c years	d generations			c wants	d can
3.	a understand	b see		**8.**	a too	b little
	c want	d hear			c to	d more
4.	a speech	b shows		**9.**	a office	b home
	c men	d women			c school	d station
5.	a wrong	b slow		**10.**	a asks	b thinks
	c fast	d bad			c wants	d says

Chapter 15

Reading Comprehension

A comprehension exercise consists of a passage upon which questions are set to test the students' ability to understand the content of the given text and to infer information and meanings from it.

Tips for Attempting Comprehension

- Read the passage fairly and quickly to get the general idea.
- Read the passage again. This time read it a little slowly, so as to know the details.
- Study the questions thoroughly.
- When answering a question, turn to the relevant portions of the passage and read them again.
- Write the answers in your own words neatly and precisely, by using complete sentences. Do not copy the text from the passage.
- If you are asked to give the meaning of any words or phrases, you should express the idea as clearly as possible in your own words.

Practice Centre

Exercise I

Read the passage carefully and select the option that you consider the most appropriate answer to each question.

Nagaland, one of India's smallest states, is located in the North-East part of India. It is bound by Myanmar on the east, Arunachal Pradesh on the north, Asom on the west and Manipur on the south. Nagaland is mostly mountainous except for the part bordering the Asom valley. Mount Saramati is the highest peak and forms a natural barrier between Nagaland and Myanmar.

The Nagas, inhabitants of Nagaland, form more than twenty tribes. *Konyak* is the largest of the Naga tribes.

Traditionally, the Nagas wear colourful tribal outfits with bamboo shields and decorated spears. They are simple at heart, are known for their festive spirit and burst into dance and music on such occasions as festivals, marriages and at harvest time.

Folk songs and ballads popular among the Nagas uphold such values as bravery, love, generosity etc. Dances are mostly woven around war themes and are performed with amazing mock war emotions. The bamboo dance is a well-known dance of the Nagas. Colourfully dressed young girls performing the bamboo dance at an incredible speed and with great accuracy present a fascinating sight.

The Nagas celebrate their festivals with great enthusiasm. Almost every Naga tribe has its own festival. *Sankarni* is the major festival of the *Zemis* tribe. This religious festival coincides with *Shivratri*. *Sekrenyi* is a festival celebrated by the *Angamis* tribe to ensure the health and well-being of the community. *Moatsu* is the most important festival celebrated by the *Aos* tribe after the sowing is over. Feasting and merry-making invariably accompany festivals.

Wood carving is a famous Naga craft. The *Konyaks*, the best wood carvers among all the Naga tribes, are skilled in carving human and animal figures. Weaving is a traditional Naga art in which each tribe has its own special designs and colours. Shawls, shoulder bags and intricately woven mats and baskets make magnificent souvenirs for tourists.

Questions

1. Naga folk dances are mostly based on the theme of ___________.
   - a harvesting
   - b religion
   - c war
   - d health

2. Which Naga tribe is having the best wood carvers?
   - a The *Angamis*
   - b The *Konyaks*
   - c The *Zemis*
   - d The *Aos*

3. Which of the following statements is <u>not</u> correct?
   - a The western part of Nagaland is not mountainous.
   - b *Moatsu* is a festival associated with agriculture.
   - c Naga girls perform the bamboo dance.
   - d The *Konyaks* are the smallest of the Naga tribes in number.

4. The word 'souvenirs' in the last paragraph means ___________.
   - a trophies or prizes
   - b some things to preserve the memory of an occasion
   - c crowns
   - d special shoes

5. A synonym for the word 'mock' used in the fourth paragraph is ___________.
   - a real
   - b laughing
   - c artificial
   - d ridiculing

Exercise II

Read the passage carefully and select the correct options in the questions given.

The presence of certain qualities makes friendship a special relationship. A true friend is not afraid to give an honest opinion and does not say things for the sake of getting appreciation. A friend provides companionship and continuous support. There is no room for pride, jealousy or rivalry in friendship.

When one enjoys a period of prosperity, many people become friends. This is not friendship because these so-called friends pull away in difficult times. True friends stand by each other both in good and difficult times. A friend in need is a friend indeed is a truism which holds true always.

Sugriva, the king of the monkey clan, was a famous character in the great Indian epic *Ramayana*. The role of *Sugriva* starts after *Sita's* kidnapping. *Sugriva* also has a similar sad tale to narrate to *Ram*, and with his help challenges *Bali*. During the war *Bali* is killed by *Ram* and *Sugriva* returns as the king of *Kishkindha*. In the *Ramayana*, *Sugriva* and *Ram* honour their pact of friendship throughout the entire epic. With the help of *Ram*, *Sugriva* kills his brother *Bali* and regains the kingdom. In return *Sugriva* provides his army to assist *Ram* in his search for *Sita* and does not rest until she is found and returned to *Ram*.

In the *Mahabharata*, *Karna*, at the cost of his own life, remains a true friend to *Duryodhana*. He honours his friendship with *Duryodhana* even after knowing that he, in reality, is the son of *Kunti* and that the *Pandavas* are his brothers. He does not break his commitment to *Duryodhana*.

Questions

1. Which of the following is the correct conduct of true friends?
   - a They appreciate each other
   - b They are afraid to give an honest opinion
   - c They are jealous of each other
   - d They stand by each other in good and difficult times

2. Why did *Karna* not break his commitment to *Duryodhana*?
   - a Because he did not want to die
   - b Because he was respecting his friendship with *Duryodhana*
   - c Because he was the son of *Kunti*
   - d All of the above

3. The word 'epic' in the third paragraph means __________.
   - a a long poem about the deeds of great people
   - b taking place over a long time period
   - c musical drama
   - d dance performance

4. The word 'rivalry' in the first paragraph means __________.
   - a quarreling
   - b consideration
   - c competition
   - d equality

5. Who is the example of a true friend in the *Ramayana*?
   - a Sita
   - b Sugriva
   - c Bali
   - d Karna

Exercise III

Read the passage carefully and select the correct options in the questions given.

Galileo

Galileo Galilei was born in the year 1564 in the town of Pisa, Italy. When he was 20 years old, he was studying in Pisa. His father wanted him to be a doctor, but Galileo was bored with school except for Maths. Because Maths was the one subject where he was doing well, the court mathematician offered to tutor him privately so he could become a qualified mathematician. Galileo's father was disappointed, but he agreed.

Because he needed to earn money, Galileo began experimenting with different things, trying to come up with some sort of invention that he could sell for money. He had a little bit of success with his invention that was like a compass that could be used to measure plots of land. He had already experimented with pendulums, thermometers and magnets.

When he heard that a Dutch inventor had invented something called a spyglass, but was keeping it a secret, Galileo decided to work on one of his own. Within 24 hours, he had invented a telescope that could magnify things to make them appear ten times larger than real life.

One night, he pointed his telescope toward the sky, and made his first of many space observations: the moon was not smooth, like everyone thought. The moon was covered with bumps and craters. As technology has improved, first Galileo, and then many others, have made improvements on the telescope, the wonderful device that allows us to see from a distance.

Questions

1. What do you understand about Galileo from the second sentence of the third paragraph?
   - a Galileo was a slow worker.
   - b Galileo wanted to become famous.
   - c Galileo could measure plots of land with his compass.
   - d Galileo was a great inventor.

2. Which of the following items had Galileo experimented with before inventing the telescope?
   - a Magnets
   - b Pendulums
   - c Thermometers
   - d All of the above

3. Which one of the following is not true, as per the passage?

  a The moon's surface is smooth.
  b Galileo's telescope made things appear ten times larger.
  c Galileo did well in the Maths subject in school.
  d Galileo designed a compass for measuring plots of land.

4. The word 'mathematician' in the first paragraph means __________.

  a a student of Maths
  b an expert in Maths
  c a person appointed to a court
  d All of the above

5. The word 'magnify' in the third paragraph means __________.

  a to make something larger
  b exaggerate
  c to make something appear larger
  d make more important

Exercise IV

Read the passage carefully and select the correct options in the questions given.

The Age of Dinosaurs

Today, human beings control Earth. Millions of years ago, before humans existed, dinosaurs ruled Earth. Their fossils have been found all over the world. They ruled Earth for 160 million years. That is much longer than people have been here. Dinosaurs became extinct long before humans existed. Humans and dinosaurs never lived at the same time. Dinosaurs ruled Earth until an unknown catastrophic event made them extinct.

Many scientists believe that a very long time ago, all of the continents were one. As time went by, the continents drifted apart. This explains why dinosaur fossils can be found all over the world. The weather was warmer and more stable than it is today. The temperature would barely rise or fall throughout the year. Therefore, there were no seasons.

Dinosaurs were not alone on the planet. Small mammals and birds existed. There were many reptiles, such as crocodiles and lizards, roaming about. Some fish, sharks, and shellfish were living as well. The Earth had many plants. There was plenty of food to go around and the Earth's creatures maintained a balanced food chain.

No one is sure why the dinosaurs became extinct. There are many theories, but none have been proven.

Questions

1. What is this passage mostly about?

  a How life would be different if dinosaurs were still alive
  b How dinosaurs ruled Earth.
  c What dinosaurs ate.
  d The age of dinosaurs before they became extinct

2. Which of the following conclusions is supported by information in the passage?

  a There was plenty of food to go around during the age of dinosaurs.
  b There was a lack of plant and animal diversity during the time of dinosaurs.
  c Dinosaurs only lived in one section of the earth.
  d Dinosaurs became extinct when humans came into existence.

3. According to the passage, it is likely that dinosaur fossils are found everywhere because

  a they lived in many different places
  b they moved around often
  c people moved the fossils around
  d the continents drifted apart

4. As used in the passage, the word 'stable' means __________.

  a uncomfortable
  b not likely to change
  c very extreme
  d threatening

5. In the sentence given below, select the option that best completes it. Dinosaur fossils have been found all over the earth by humans __________ the continents drifted apart after dinosaurs became extinct.

  a even though   b however
  c because   d yet

Exercise V

Read the passage carefully and select the correct options in the questions given.

Taiga Ecosystems

The weather is very cold in taiga ecosystems. The winter season lasts a long time, and the weather is icy cold. Storms are severe, bringing biting cold winds. Summers never get very warm and the summer season is exceptionally short. There isn't much precipitation in a taiga ecosystem. When moisture does fall, it usually comes in the form of dry, powdery snow.

Living in the extreme conditions of a taiga ecosystem takes a special kind of organism. Some common animals you could find in the area are moose, wolves, and deer. Each population must adapt to the severe conditions. Short, stubby grass and shrubs grow in taiga regions, but they are better known for their beautiful evergreen trees. All the trees you think of when you imagine kinds of Christmas trees are at home in the taiga. Pines, firs, and spruce trees are common. The thin, waxy leaves (sometimes called needles) of evergreen trees hold in water all year round. They also do not freeze easily, even when the temperatures drop down low. Like all green plants, the trees of the taiga region are an important source of oxygen for our planet. As they go through the process of photosynthesis to make their food, green plants "breathe" out oxygen into the air. Since taiga ecosystems have so many trees, they help make up for areas with less vegetation, like the desert.

Taiga ecosystems cover large areas of North America, Europe, and Asia. A good example of a taiga ecosystem in the United States is the state of Alaska.

People living and working in taiga regions often disrupt the natural balance. Activities such as hunting, trapping and fishing affect the animal populations, sometimes thinning them to the point that they are endangered. Mining for oil and gas and harvesting trees does irreparable damage, destroying animal habitats and robbing the Earth of important oxygen sources. Even tourism can be damaging, as many tourists do not respect wildlife and plants, being willing to sacrifice them for developed recreational areas. Of course people have the right to use natural resources, but they must do it in a way that makes resources renewable and does not harm the environment.

Questions

1. Which of the following best describes the seasons in a taiga ecosystem?
   a The winter is very cold and long, while the summer is short and slightly warm.
   b There is heavy rain in winter and the summer is hot.
   c Snow falls in the winter and rain falls in the summer.
   d None of the above

2. What characteristic of the trees in the taiga is well known?
   a The tree trunks are very tall.
   b They are evergreen with thin waxy leaves.
   c The trees shed their leaves in winter.
   d The trees do not use photosynthesis for making their food.

3. Which human activities disrupt the natural balance of the taiga ecosystems?
   a Planting new trees
   b Using natural resources in a way that makes resources renewable
   c Not damaging animal habitats
   d Hunting, trapping and fishing

4. The phrase 'biting cold' in the first paragraph means __________.
   a cold which can be tolerated
   b warm
   c very cold and unpleasant
   d None of the above

5. The word 'irreparable' in the fourth paragraph means __________.
   a drastic
   b too serious to put right
   c slight
   d None of these

Exercise VI

Read the passage carefully and select the correct options in the questions given.

Spotted Cats

Several members of the cat family have spotted fur. Do you know the difference between a leopard, a jaguar, and a cheetah? From a distance they may appear somewhat similar. Examined at closer range, however, they are clearly different cats. They differ in various ways, including where they live, how big they are, how they move and hunt, and how their fur is marked.

Of all the big cats in the wild, the true leopard is found across the largest area. Leopards live in much of Asia and Africa. A leopard grows to be from 3 to 6 feet long, with an added 3 feet of tail. Leopards are skilled climbers that can hunt monkeys in trees. They can also lie in wait and pounce on passing prey. When food sources are scarce, they might eat fruit, field mice, and large insects. Leopard spots are not actually solid spots; they are broken circles.

The jaguar is native to the Americas. Its natural range is from the southern United States to northern Argentina, with the largest concentration of jaguars being in Brazil and Central America. The beauty and power of the jaguar inspired worship among ancient peoples. It measures between 3 and 6 feet long without the tail, which adds another 1½ to 2½ feet. Possessing a large head and body, the jaguar has legs that are shorter and thicker than a leopard's. Jaguars are excellent climbers and can also swim well. They dine on a variety of land, tree, and water creatures. Their fur can be a vivid yellow colour or a rusty shade; their "spots" are called rosettes. Each rosette is large and black, consisting of a middle spot with a circle of spots around it.

Most cheetahs live in the wilds of Africa. There are also some in Iran and Northwestern Afghanistan. The cheetah's head is smaller than the leopard's, and its body is longer. This cat is built for speed. Its legs are much longer than the leopard's, allowing it to run at speeds of up to 70 miles per hour! This incredible ability helps the cheetahs catch their dinner, which is usually an unfortunate antelope. A cheetah's spots are simply black spots, not rosettes or circles.

Other spotted cats include the smaller ocelot, mainly of Central and South America, and the lynx or bobcat, mainly of North America. What all of these cats have in common is that they are wild, powerful animals of tremendous grace and beauty.

Questions

1. Which of the following is the best summary of this passage?
   a All spotted cats are powerful, beautiful, and graceful.
   b There are many different spotted cats in the world.
   c Spotted cats may look similar, but they are different in many ways.
   d Spotted cats in the wild hunt many different kinds of animals.

2. Which of the following is not a way to tell the difference between spotted cats?
   a How beautiful they are
   b Where they live
   c What their spots look like
   d How big they are

3. Which of the following words from the passage express an attitude of sympathy for animals attacked by spotted cats?
   a . . . that they are wild, powerful animals . . .
   b . . . might eat fruit, field mice, and large insects.
   c . . . how they move and hunt . . .
   d . . . dinner, which is usually an unfortunate antelope.

4. The word 'prey' in the third paragraph means __________ .
   a disturbance   b victim
   c killer   d attacker

5. The word 'wilds' in the fifth paragraph means __________ .
   a jungles
   b uncivilised
   c far from cities and towns
   d angry

Exercise VII

Read the passage carefully and select the correct options in the questions given.

One January day, on his usual begging tour, he tramped despondently up and down the region round about Mincing Lane and Little East Cheap, hour after hour, bare-footed and cold, looking in at cook-shop windows and longing for the dreadful pork-pies and other deadly inventions displayed there — for to him these were dainties fit for the angels; that is, judging by the smell, they were — for it had never been his good luck to own and eat one. There was a cold drizzle of rain; the atmosphere was murky; it was a melancholy day.

At night Tom reached home so wet and tired and hungry that it was not possible for his father and grandmother to observe his forlorn condition and not be moved — after their fashion; wherefore they gave him a brisk cuffing at once and sent him to bed. For a long time his pain and hunger, and the swearing and fighting going on in the building, kept him awake; but at last his thoughts drifted away to far, romantic lands, and he fell asleep in the company of jewelled and gilded princelings who live in vast palaces, and had servants *salaaming* before them or flying to execute their orders. And then, as usual, he dreamed that he was a princeling himself.

All night long the glories of his royal estate shone upon him; he moved among great lords and ladies, in a blaze of light, breathing perfumes, drinking in delicious music, and answering the reverent obeisances of the glittering throng as it parted to make way for him, with here a smile, and there a nod of his princely head.

And when he awoke in the morning and looked upon the wretchedness about him, his dream had had its usual effect — it had intensified the sordidness of his surroundings a thousandfold. Then came bitterness, and heart-break, and tears.

Questions

1. How is Tom's real life different from his dream regarding the people he moved with?
- a In reality he moves with his father and grandmother, while in his dreams he moves with servants.
- b In reality he moves alone (begging), while in his dreams he moves among great lords and ladies.
- c In reality he moves among great lords and ladies while in his dreams he moves alone (begging).
- d There is no difference.

2. Why did Tom cry on waking up in the morning?
- a Because his father had beaten him.
- b Because he was afraid that he will not get anything to eat today.
- c Because he was sad at his pitiful state in life.
- d None of the above

3. Which one of the following is true, as per the passage?
- a Tom had very sad dreams.
- b Tom was lucky to have eaten pork-pies.
- c Tom's father and grandmother were kind to him.
- d Tom was a beggar.

4. The word 'despondently' in the first paragraph means __________.
- a sadly
- b anxiously
- c joyfully
- d happily

5. The word 'execute' in the second paragraph means __________.
- a remove
- b legally punish
- c kill
- d carry out

Exercise VIII

Read the passage carefully and select the correct options in the questions given.

One day a cat dies due to old age and goes to heaven. There she meets the lord God himself. The lord tells the cat, "You've lived a good life and if there is any way I can make your stay in heaven more comfortable, please let me know." The cat thinks for a moment and says, "Lord, all my life I have lived with a poor family and had to sleep on the hard wooden floor. Can I have a pillow to sleep on?" The lord stops the cat and says, "Say no more", and a wonderful fluffy pillow appears.

A few days later six mice were killed in a tragic farming accident and go to heaven. Again, the lord God is there to greet them with a similar offer. The mice answer, "All of our lives we have been chased by all kinds of creatures. We had to run away from cats, dogs and even women with brooms. Running, running and running, we are tired of running. Do you think we could have roller skates so that we don't have to run anymore?" The lord God says, "Say no more", and fits each mouse with beautiful new roller skates.

About a week later, the lord God stops by to see the cat and finds her in a deep sleep on the pillow. The lord gently wakes the cat and asks her, "How are things since you arrived?" The cat stretches, yawns and then replies, "It's wonderful here! In fact, it is much better than I could have expected! And those little meals on wheels you've been sending by are the best!"

Questions

1. The mice were tired of __________.
   a eating whatever they could get
   b searching for new places to live
   c looking for work
   d getting chased by everyone

2. What did the cat ask God for?
   a A mouse to eat every day.
   b Send her back to earth.
   c Give her a comfortable pillow to sleep on.
   d Make the world a better place to live.

3. What will be a suitable title for this story?
   a God is great
   b The tired mice
   c Tom and Jerry
   d Cat in heaven

4. Which of the following is an antonym of the word 'fluffy' in the passage?
   a Rough
   b Hard
   c Woolly
   d Messy

5. Which of the following is the meaning of 'deep' in the passage?
   a Sound
   b Blissful
   c Relaxing
   d Obscure

Chapter 16

Writing Skills

We will cover the following formats of composition which are usually asked in examinations:
1. Notice
2. Letters – informal and formal

Notice

A notice is used to convey information about functions, events or occasions, or used to announce something that has happened or is about to happen. Notices are generally displayed in prominent places.

The format of a typical notice is shown below.

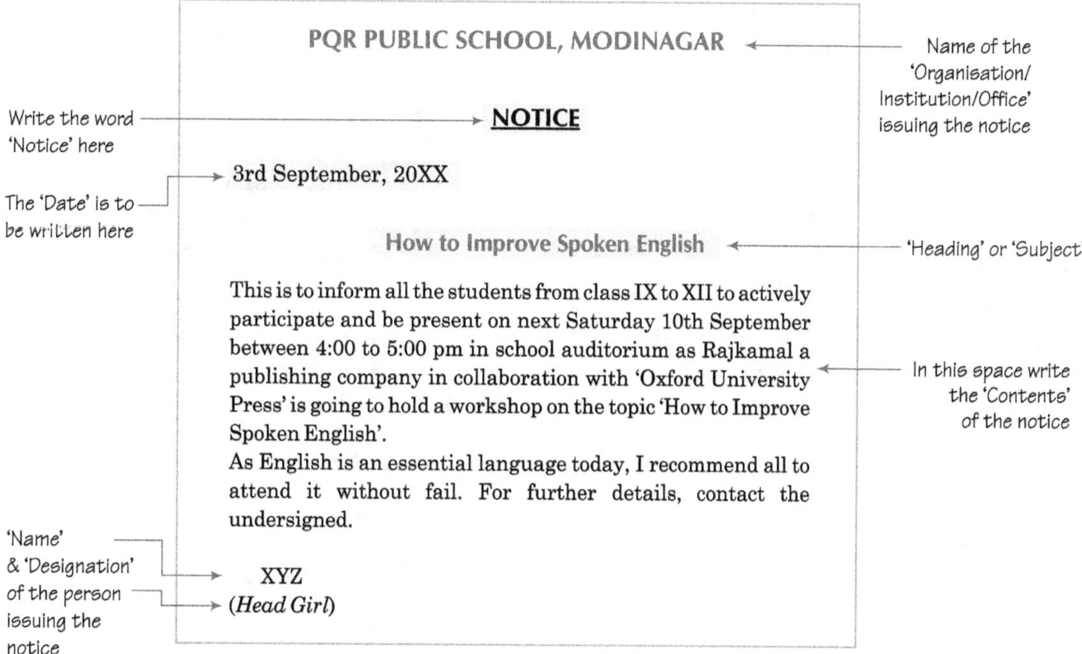

Practice Centre

Exercise I

A. A notice is given below with some parts missing, but substituted by numbers 1 to 7. Identify the numbers by selecting the correct options from those given below.

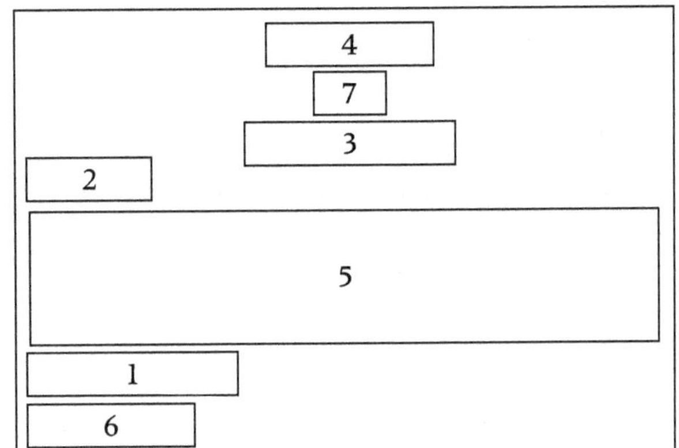

1. The item identified as '1' is
   a Name of the organisation
   b Name of issuer of the notice
   c Subject of the notice
   d Designation of issuer of the notice

2. The item identified as '2' is
   a Subject of the notice
   b Designation of issuer of the notice
   c Contents of the notice
   d Date of the notice

3. The item identified as '3' is
   a Name of the Organisation

   b The word 'NOTICE'
   c Subject of the notice
   d Date of the notice

4. The item identified as '4' is
   a Subject of the notice
   b Designation of issuer of the notice
   c Name of the organisation
   d The word 'NOTICE'

5. The item identified as '5' is
   a Date of the notice
   b Name of issuer of the notice
   c Subject of the notice
   d Contents of the notice

6. The item identified as '6' is
   a Designation of issuer of the notice
   b Name of issuer of the notice
   c Date of the notice
   d Name of the organisation

7. The item identified as '7' is
   a Date of the notice
   b The word 'NOTICE'
   c Subject of the notice
   d Name of the organisation

B. A notice by the Principal of a school is given below with some parts missing, but numbered 8 to 12. The words / phrases corresponding to these numbers are given in the options of the questions below the notice. Match the numbers with the words / phrases by selecting the options accordingly.

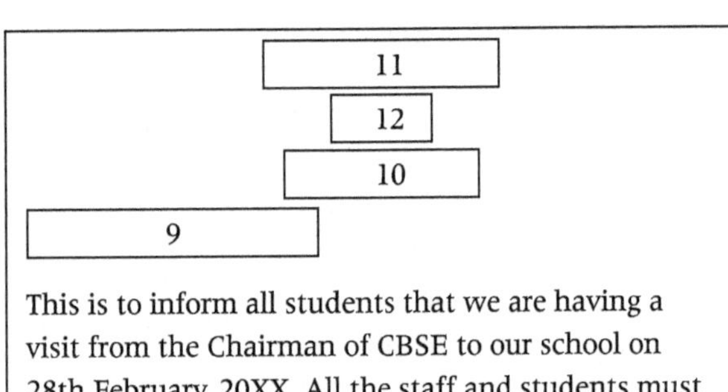

This is to inform all students that we are having a visit from the Chairman of CBSE to our school on 28th February, 20XX. All the staff and students must be well turned out on that day. With the cooperation of all, we expect to get a favourable report from the Chairman on the functioning of our school.

8. The item identified as '8' is
   a Principal
   b Chairman CBSE
   c Visitor
   d 23rd February, 20XX

9. The item identified as '9' is
   a Dear staff and students
   b Important Visitor
   c 23rd February, 20XX
   d Ambedkar Memorial School

10. The item identified as '10' is
    a NOTICE
    b 23rd February, 20XX
    c Ambedkar Memorial School
    d Important Visitor

11. The item identified as '11' is
- a 23rd February, 20XX
- b Ambedkar Memorial School
- c Important Visitor
- d NOTICE

12. The item identified as '12' is
- a Ambedkar Memorial School
- b NOTICE
- c 23rd February, 20XX
- d Principal

Letters

Letters are broadly classified into **formal** and **informal** letters.

Formal letters include

- Business letters – enquiries asking for quotations, their replies, placing orders etc.
- Official letters – conveying information to people holding office
- Applications for jobs
- Letters to editors of newspapers / magazines
- Complaints to authorities for redress

and so on.

The format of a formal letter is given below as an example.

B-168, Vivek Vihar Near Shivam Optical Delhi-110094	**Letter writer's address** *Sender's address is written here. Never put your name here*
16th December, 20XX	**Date** *The date appears directly below the address after leaving a line*
The Account Manager State Bank of India Vivek Vihar Branch Delhi- 110094	**Receiver's name/rank and his/her address**
Subject *Request for Opening a New Savings Bank Account*	**Subject of the letter** *Indicate the Theme/Subject here*
Dear Sir,	**Salutation** *It is a customary greeting with which the sender opens the letter*
This is to inform you that I, Sriram Awasthy, am interested in opening a new Saving Account in your bank. I am a permanent resident of Vivek Vihar. I am enclosing the required documents and photographs as required by you. I would appreciate it if it is opened at an early date.	**Body of the letter** *Always change the para while making a new point.*
Thanking you. *Yours sincerely* *Sriram Awasthy*	**Subscription and Signature** *Closing expression, Name and designation, if applicable*
Enclosures : *1. Copy of Aadhar card* *2. Completed application form* *3. Two Photographs*	

Informal letters include personal letters to

- Relatives
- Friends and acquaintances
- Colleagues

and so on.

The format of an informal letter is given below as an example.

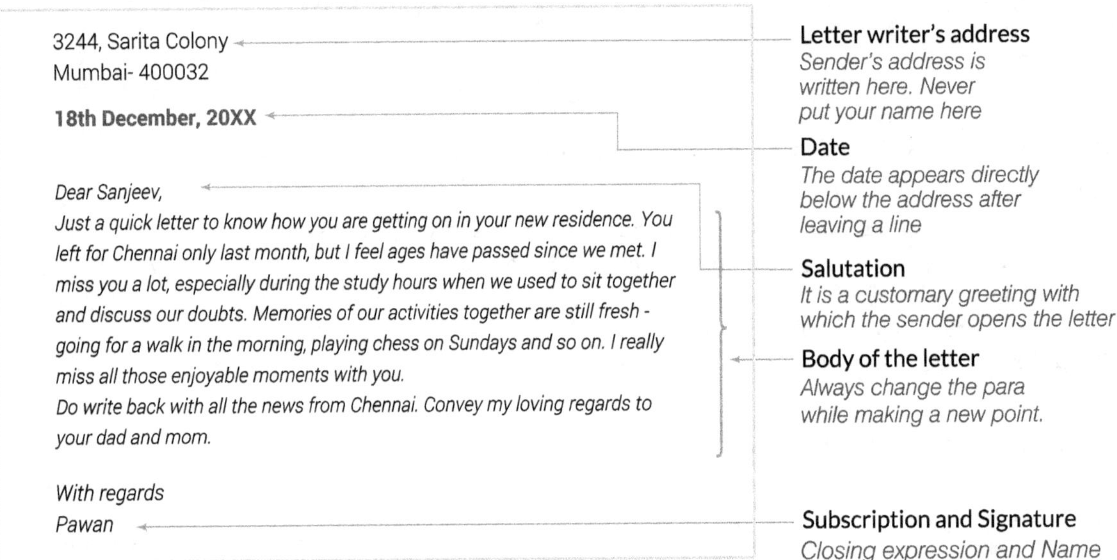

Exercise II

A. The parts of a formal letter are identified by numbers in the blank official letter format given below.

1. The item identified as '1' is
     a sender's address   b subject of letter   c salutation   d date

2. The item identified as '2' is
     a receiver's name   b receiver's address   c body of letter   d salutation

3. The item identified as '3' is
     a sender's address   b signature   c salutation   d date

4. The item identified as '4' is
     a sender's name and designation   b subscription
     c subject of letter   d date

5. The item identified as '5' is
     a sender's address   b receiver's address   c salutation   d receiver's name/rank

B. Mohan has written to his uncle thanking him for the gift he got from the uncle. This letter is given below with some parts missing, but numbered 6, 7, 8, 9 and 10. The words / phrases corresponding to these numbers are given in the options of the questions below the letter. Match the numbers with the words / phrases by selecting the options accordingly.

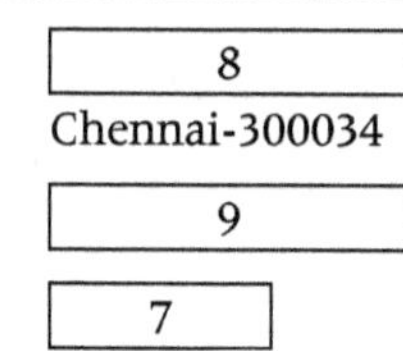

8

Chennai-300034

9

7

I received your lovely present yesterday on the occasion of my birthday. How kind of you to remember me on this day with such a nice token of your great love for me! The wrist watch you have sent me will stand me in good stead. I was often late for school and had to pay a fine every month. Now I shall be in time. Moreover, it will help me in my studies, particularly during the examination days.

6

10

6. The item identified as '6' is

  a Mohan   b Yours affectionately

  c Love to Shashi   d 12th December, 20XX

7. The item identified as '7' is

  a My dear Uncle   b December, 20XX

  c 87, Subhash Park   d Yours affectionately

8. The item identified as '8' is

  a Yours affectionately   b My dear Uncle

  c 87, Subhash Park   d Mohan

9. The item identified as '9' is

  a Love to Shashi   b 87, Subhash Park

  c My dear Uncle   d 12th December, 20XX

10. The item identified as '10' is

  a With regards   b Yours affectionately

  c Mohan   d 12th December, 20XX

Practice Sets

Practice Set ①

A Whole Content Based Test for Class 6th English Olympiad

Direction for Q nos 1-5 *Read the passage carefully and select the correct options in the questions given.*

A thief once hired a room at an inn and stayed there with the intentions of stealing some things. The next day when he was thinking of what to do next, he looked out of the window and saw the owner of the inn sitting in the courtyard. Looking closely, he realised that the owner was wearing an expensive new coat, which the thief decided would look good on himself. To give fruit to his plan, the thief went and sat next to the innkeeper. Striking up a conversation, he got talking about things which were of no interest to either of the two.

During the conversation, to the innkeeper's astonishment, he yawned and then howled like a wolf. The innkeeper was curious and asked him as to why did he do that? The thief said he had no control over his yawning and if he yawned three times, he actually turned into a wolf. He begged the innkeeper not to leave him, as he was frightened. Moreover, with that he yawned again and let out another howl. The innkeeper turned pale and got up to go, but the thief caught hold of his coat and begged him to stay. Even as he pleaded, he yawned again. The terrified innkeeper wriggled out of the coat to which the thief was tightly holding on, ran into the inn, and locked himself in. The thief calmly put on the coat and walked away.

Questions

1. What did the thief want to do?
    - a Stay at the inn without paying.
    - b Steal the innkeeper's coat.
    - c Change into a wolf.
    - d Talk to the innkeeper.

2. The thief turning into a wolf was __________.
    - a an actual fact
    - b in the innkeeper's imagination
    - c a story for tourists
    - d a story made up by the thief

3. What will be a suitable title of the story?
    - a A scared innkeeper
    - b The thief who became a wolf
    - c The intelligent thief
    - d The tempting coat

4. Which of the following is the synonym of the word 'curious' in the passage?
    - a Interested
    - b Strange
    - c Surprising
    - d Ordinary

5. Which word in the passage means the same as 'desires'?
    - a Requirements
    - b Interest
    - c Things
    - d Intentions

Direction for Q nos 6–7 *Select the option which is an antonym of the word underlined in the sentence given.*

6. Girish was feeling <u>triumphant</u> when he stood first in class.
    - a despondent
    - b sad
    - c happy
    - d victorious

7. Shubham is an <u>arrogant</u> person as he never listens to anyone but himself.
    - a poor
    - b inferior
    - c modest
    - d superior

6
9
8
7
10

8. The item identified as '6' is
   a Subject of the notice
   b Designation of issuer of the notice
   c Contents of the notice
   d Name of the organisation

9. The item identified as '7' is
   a Date of the notice
   b Subject of the notice
   c Contents of the notice
   d Designation of issuer of the notice

10. The item identified as '8' is
   a Name of the Organisation
   b Name of issuer of the notice
   c Subject of the notice
   d Date of the notice

11. The item identified as '9' is
   a Date of the notice
   b Name of issuer of the notice
   c Subject of the notice
   d Contents of the notice

12. The item identified as '10' is
   a Name of the organisation
   b Name of issuer of the notice
   c Subject of the notice
   d Designation of issuer of the notice

Direction for Q nos 13–14 *Fill in the blanks with the correct determiners from the options given.*

13. Although Sudhir is very ill, he didn't take __________ medicine.
   a much   b many
   c any   d lots of

14. The shoes you have purchased yesterday are more durable than __________ you bought last year.
   a those   b these
   c this   d that

Direction for Q nos 15-16 *Choose the right modal verb from the options given to fill in the blanks.*

15. "Do you think it ________ rain today?" (expressing a possibility or a wish)
   a might   b will
   c could   d may

16. "Kavita, You ________ finish your chapaties and vegetables before you have the ice cream." (expressing a command)
   a would   b can
   c may   d must

Directions for Q nos 17–18 *Select the option which is a synonym of the word given.*

17. Enchanting
   a Spell   b Magic
   c Captivating   d Ugly

18. Ingenuity
   a Foolishness   b Quietness
   c Originality   d Quickness

Directions for Q nos 19–20 *Fill in the blanks with suitable active or passive verb forms from the options given.*

19. The Taj Mahal __________ (visit) by millions of people this year.
   a will visit
   b will be visited
   c is visited
   d has been visiting

20. Ramesh __________ (read, not) the writing of the teacher on the blackboard.
   a could not be read
   b could not read
   c not reading
   d will not have read

Practice Set 1

21. "Rashid and Salma, stop talking in the class", said the teacher.

    a The teacher asked Rashid and Salma when they would stop talking in the class.

    b The teacher did not want Rashid to talk to Salma in the class.

    c The teacher forbade Salma to talk with Rashid in the class.

    d The teacher told Rashid and Salma to stop talking in the class.

22. "Will you please meet me at the airport?" said Rajendra to me on the telephone.

    a Rajendra commanded me on the telephone to meet him at the airport.

    b Rajendra wanted to know from me on the telephone whether I could meet him at the airport.

    c Rajendra requested me on the telephone to meet him at the airport.

    d Rajendra wanted me to meet him at the airport on the telephone.

Direction for Q nos 23-24 *Fill in the blanks with the most appropriate prepositions and accordingly select the best option.*

23. "Rakesh, will you please shut the door _____ you?"

    a off   **b** before

    c behind   **d** along

24. Balwinder has qualified _____ the post _____ Security Supervisor.

    a for, of   **b** of, in

    c for, of   **d** at, by

Direction for Q nos 25–26 *In the passage below, the first and last sentences are identified as A and Z. The remaining four sentences are labelled as P, Q, R and S. Find the correct sequence of these four sentences and select the correct option accordingly.*

25.   A Karan was called for a job interview.

    P The interviewer was impressed by Karan's sense of cleanliness.

    Q In the corridor he saw a piece of waste paper lying on the floor.

    R He went to the place of interview.

    S Karan picked it up and threw it in the dustbin.

    Z Karan got the job.

    a PQRS   **b** QPSR

    c RQSP   **d** QRPS

26.   A Ashok woke up one morning to a beautiful sunrise.

    P Ashok had two fried eggs and four slices of buttered toast.

    Q He was feeling very hungry this morning.

    R So he hurried to the breakfast table after brushing his teeth.

    S In addition, he drank a large glass of milk to go with them.

    Z After the breakfast he reached the bus stop to catch his school bus.

    a PQRS   **b** QPSR   **c** RPQS   **d** QRPS

Direction for Q nos 27-30 *Fill in the blanks with the correct tense of the verb given in brackets immediately after the blank and accordingly select the best option.*

27. All the people _____ (wait) for this day for a long time.

    a had been waiting   **b** has been waiting

    c were been waiting   **d** were waited

28. The train _____ (leave) Nagpur station at 6 PM.

    a was left   **b** had left

    c had leaved   **d** has leaved

29. Polar explorers _________ (explore) Antarctica since the beginning of the twentieth century.

    a will be exploring   **b** has explored

    c had exploring   **d** have been exploring

30. Our team _________ (discuss) about the water shortage with the villagers.

    a were discussed   **b** will discussed

    c was discussing   **d** would discussing

Answers

1. b	2. d	3. c	4. a	5. d	6. a	7. c	8. d	9. c	10. d
11. c	12. b	13. c	14. a	15. b	16. d	17. c	18. c	19. b	20. b
21. d	22. c	23. c	24. a	25. c	26. d	27. a	28. b	29. d	30. c

Practice Set ②

A Whole Content Based Test for Class 6th English Olympiad

Directions for Q nos 1-5 *Read the passage carefully and select the option that you consider the most appropriate answer to each question given below the passage.*

Ghiyasuddin Tughlaq was the son of a Turkish father and an Indian mother. He was an efficient administrator and a capable military commander. He introduced several reforms for the welfare of his subjects and suppressed revolts in distant provinces. He restored peace and stability in the Delhi Sultanate. Ghiyasuddin died in what appeared to be a deliberately planned accident. He was succeeded by his son, Jauna Khan, who ascended the throne under the title of Muhammad bin Tughlaq.

It is said that Muhammad bin Tughlaq erected a splendid pavilion to welcome his father home from a military campaign. However, the pavilion was designed to collapse when struck by elephants passing in parade. Ghiyasuddin was killed and his son succeeded him.

Muhammad bin Tughlaq was one of the most learned and accomplished scholars of his time. His intellectual curiosity and thirst for knowledge were boundless. Gifted with an extraordinary memory and a keen intellect, he had mastered logic, philosophy, mathematics, astronomy and physical sciences. He was a lover of Persian literature as well as poetry, calligraphy, fine arts and music. He loved the company of learned men.

Historians are divided on the nature of his character. The contradictions in his character have led some historians to believe that he was mad. He has been variously described as the wisest fool, a madman, an idealist and a visionary.

He was a diligent ruler and undertook many projects. These projects were brilliantly conceived but poorly executed and always ended in failure

Questions

1. How did Ghiyasuddin Tughlaq die?
    a He died in an accident.
    b He may have been murdered.
    c He died of old age.
    d He died fighting for his kingdom.

2. Why do some historians think that Muhammad bin Tughlaq was mad?
    a His actions were unbecoming of a king.
    b He made brilliant plans which failed.
    c Because of the number of contradictions in his character.
    d He took up many useless projects.

3. Which of the following is not true of Ghiyasuddin as a ruler?
    a He introduced many reforms.
    b He was a brave commander.
    c He was a good military commander.
    d He did not care for his subjects.

4. The word 'boundless' in the third paragraph means __________.
    a without limits
    b continuous
    c not reachable
    d cunning

5. The word 'diligent' in the last paragraph means __________.
    a intelligent
    b tireless
    c painstaking
    d cunning

6. The item identified as '6' is
    a sender's address   b subscription
    c salutation   d date

7. The item identified as '7' is
    a receiver's name   b receiver's address
    c body of letter   d theme of letter

8. The item identified as '8' is
    a sender's address   b signature
    c salutation   d date

9. The item identified as '9' is
    a sender's name / rank
    b body of letter
    c subject of letter
    d subscription

10. The item identified as '10' is
    a receiver's name / rank
    b receiver's address
    c salutation
    d theme of letter

Direction for Q nos 11–12 *Fill in the blanks with the correct determiners from the options given.*

11. _______ birds sing in ________ tree every morning.
    a That, this   b Those, that
    c Those, these   d These, these

12. Do you understand ________ words?
    a those   b these   c this   d that

Direction for Q nos 13–14 *Select the option which is a synonym of the word underlined in the sentence given.*

13. It was a <u>miracle</u> that Madhu was alive, after the fall she had from the roof of our home.
    a illusion b wonder c joyful d funny

14. Palit is an <u>immature</u> man for his age.
    a childish   b unripe
    c unfinished   d ancient

Direction for Q nos 15-16 *Choose the right modal verb from the options given to fill in the blanks.*

15. I asked my friends to help me move because I knew that I _____ fit all my possessions into my little car. (inability)
    a don't be able to   b can't be able to
    c not be able to   d couldn't

16. I know that everyone _______ save a little extra money, but it is hard with so many bills to pay. (customary, expected behaviour)
    a was able to   b could have
    c is supposed to   d must

Direction for Q nos 17–18 *Fill in the blanks with the most appropriate prepositions and accordingly select the best option.*

17. Basmati rice is sold ______ the nearby shop ______ Rs 40 per kilo.
    a at, of   b in, at
    c above, up   d for, to

18. Rajesh was willing ______ agree ______ Sharmila's suggestion ______ seeing the new movie.
    a for, for, for   b to, to, to
    c to, of, in   d to, to, for

Directions for Q nos 19-20 *Convert the active to passive verb form or vice-versa and select the correct option.*

19. Somebody told me that there was an explosion in a local train in Kolkata.
    a I was told by somebody about the explosion in a local train in Kolkata.
    b I was told about the explosion in a local train in Kolkata.
    c I was informed that there was an explosion in a local train in Kolkata.
    d I was told by somebody that there had been an explosion in a local train in Kolkata.

Practice Set 2

20. Did the loud noise frighten you?

    a Were you frighten by the loud noise?

    b Was you frightened by the loud noise?

    c Did you frighten the loud noise?

    d Were you frightened by the loud noise?

21. Select the option in indirect speech which correctly expresses the sentence given. Gaurav said to Sunita, "Will you please help me in my work just now?"

    a Gaurav requested Sunita to help him in his work just then.

    b Gaurav questioned Sunita that will you please help me in my work just now.

    c Gaurav told Sunita whether she will help him in his work just now.

    d Gaurav asked to Sunita that will she please help him in his work just now.

22. Select the option in direct speech which correctly expresses the sentence given. The motorist enquired of the farmer if he could tell him the way to the nearest restaurant.

    a The motorist said to the farmer, "Can you tell me where is the nearest restaurant?"

    b The motorist said to the farmer, "Can you tell me the way to the nearest restaurant?"

    c The motorist said to the farmer, "Where is the nearest restaurant?"

    d The motorist said to the farmer, "Which is the way to the nearest restaurant?"

Direction for Q nos 23–24 *Choose the correct modal verb from the options given to fill in the blanks.*

23. __________ 3 PM suit you?

    a Should   b Would   c Shall   d Ought

24. __________ I have one more ice cream, Mum?

    a Will   b May   c Must   d Would

Direction for Q nos 25–26 *Select the option which is an antonym of the word underlined in the sentence given.*

25. Karan was so <u>lazy</u> that he did not even get up from the chair to answer the doorbell.

    a inactive b smart   c active   d tired

26. Satyendra was <u>praised</u> by the teacher for standing first in the class.

    a insulted   b approved

    c adored   d criticised

Direction for Q nos 27-28 *Fill in the blanks with the correct tense of the verb given in brackets immediately after the blank and accordingly select the best option.*

27. When Lalit ______ (wake up) his mother______ (already / prepare) breakfast

    a had woken up, already preparing

    b woke up, had already prepared

    c waking up, prepared already

    d wake up, already prepare

28. Sharmila usually ______ (put) on black shoes but now she ______ (wear) white sandals.

    a puts, is wearing   b putting, wears

    c put, wear   d has put, is worn

Direction for Q nos 29–30 *In the passage below, the first and last sentences are identified as A and Z. The remaining four sentences are labelled as P, Q, R and S. Find the correct sequence of these four sentences and select the correct option accordingly.*

29. A A dog stole a piece of chicken from a restaurant.

    P It crossed a river on the way to the jungle.

    Q Thinking it was another dog, it barked at it in anger.

    R It put the chicken in its mouth and ran out to the jungle.

    S It saw its reflection in the river water.

    Z It lost the piece of chicken as it fell in the river.

    a PQRS   b RQPS   c RPSQ   d QRPS

30. A Ram and Rahim were two poor boys in a village.

    P However, they wanted regular work, as they were poor.

    Q On other days they did not have any work.

    R Both of them worked as labourers in the weekly market on Sundays.

    S So the village Sarpanch employed them to help in his farming.

    Z Thus both the boys found regular work.

    a PQRS   b QPSR   c RPQS   d RQPS

Answers

1. b	2. c	3. d	4. a	5. c	6. a	7. c	8. d	9. c	10. a
11. b	12. b	13. b	14. a	15. d	16. c	17. b	18. d	19. c	20. d
21. a	22. b	23. b	24. b	25. c	26. d	27. b	28. a	29. c	30. d

Practice Set 2

Practice Set 3

A Whole Content Based Test for Class 6th English Olympiad

Direction for Q nos 1-5 *Read the passage carefully and select the option that you consider the most appropriate answer to each question given below the passage.*

Once a man saw three masons along with some labourers who were constructing a temple. He observed the masons for some days and found that though the three of them were doing the same kind of work, there was a marked difference in their approach to their job.

He saw that the first mason reported for his work late, did his work half-heartedly and sluggishly enjoyed longer rest intervals, frequently checked the time on his wrist-watch and left the work before time. The second mason was very punctual in arriving and leaving, and did his work methodically and conscientiously. The third mason, however, would come before time, took few intervals and often worked overtime.

The man naturally got curious and wanted to know the three masons' outlook towards their work. He asked them what they were doing. The first mason tapped his protruding belly with his hand and said, "I am earning fuel for this belly." The second said, "I am constructing a building." The third looked at the stately building and said "I am building the house of God."

Questions

1. The writer is trying to tell the readers that __________.

    a all work and no play is healthy
    b all play and no work is healthy
    c enjoy doing work with commitment
    d All of the above

2. The first mason's approach to work was that of __________.

    a earning his livelihood b passing the time
    c earning only money d wasting time

3. The third mason approached his work with __________.

    a eagerness b skill
    c duty d dedication

4. The phrase, 'work is worship' can be associated with __________.

    a the first mason b the second mason
    c the third mason d all the three masons

5. Which word from the passage means the opposite of 'vigorously'?

    a conscientiously (paragraph 2)
    b sluggishly (paragraph 2)
    c half-heartedly (paragraph 2)
    d stately (paragraph 3)

Direction for Q nos 6–8 *Fill in the blanks with the correct determiners from the options given.*

6. You cannot ride __________ horses because thcy are too weak with hunger.
    a these b this
    c that d an

7. "How __________ students are there in Section A of our class?" asked the teacher of Section B.
    a all b any
    c some d many

8. __________ chocolate ice cream is delicious!
    a That b This
    c These d Those

Direction for Q nos 9–10 *Select the option which is a synonym of the word underlined in the sentence given.*

9. Cricket crazy fans <u>worship</u> Sachin for his wonderful batting.
    a adore b revere
    c love d like

10. The German army <u>retreated</u> in the face of the strong attack by the Allies during the Second World War.
    a failed b hide
    c delivered d withdrew

```
________________6________________
_________________________________
________7________
____8____                              9
_________________________________
_________________________________
_________________________________
________10________
_________________________________
```

11. The item identified as '6' is
  a sender's address   b subscription
  c salutation   d date

12. The item identified as '7' is
  a receiver's name   b receiver's address
  c body of letter   d date

13. The item identified as '8' is
  a sender's address   b signature
  c salutation   d date

14. The item identified as '9' is
  a sender's name / rank
  b body of letter
  c subject of letter
  d subscription

15. The item identified as '10' is
  a receiver's name / rank
  b receiver's address
  c salutation
  d subscription

Direction for Q nos 16–17 *Select the option which is an antonym of the word underlined in the sentence given.*

16. Surojit was <u>alive</u> when we removed him from the debris of the collapsed building.
  a unconscious   b asleep
  c sleeping   d dead

17. Porus had to <u>retreat</u> when his army was defeated by Alexander's army.
  a progress   b decline
  c advance   d grow

Direction for Q nos 18-19 *Choose the right modal verb from the options given to fill in the blanks.*

18. "You _______ for me; I could have found the way by myself."
  a couldn't wait
  b didn't wait
  c needn't have waited
  d might not wait

19. Sarita was afraid that if she asked Jai Prakash again, he _______ refuse again.
  a can   b might
  c would surely   d may

Directions for Q nos 20–21 *Convert the passive to active verb form or vice-versa and select the correct option.*

20. Students often borrow school library books.
  a School students often borrow books from the library.
  b Students are in the habit of borrowing books from the school library.
  c Books from the library are often borrowed by school students.
  d School library books are often borrowed by students.

21. Prime Minister Modi was welcomed by the people.
  a People welcomed Prime Minister Modi.
  b The people welcome Prime Minister Modi.
  c The people welcoming Prime Minister Modi.
  d The people welcomed Prime Minister Modi.

Direction for Q nos 22–23 *Select the option in indirect speech which correctly expresses the sentence given.*

22. "I went for a long drive on my scooter yesterday", said Kalpana.
  a Kalpana said that she had gone for a long drive on her scooter the day before.
  b Kalpana said that I went for a long drive on my scooter yesterday.
  c Kalpana said that I went for a long drive on my scooter the other day.
  d Kalpana said that she went for a long drive on my scooter just yesterday.

Practice Set 3

23. "How clever I am!" Rashid said. "All my life I have been talking in poetry without knowing it."

    a Rashid said that he was very clever. All his life he was talking in poetry without knowing it.

    b Rashid exclaimed that he was very clever. All his life he had been talking in poetry without knowing it.

    c Rashid said that how clever he was. All his life he had been talking in poetry without knowing it.

    d Rashid exclaimed how clever I am. All my life he had been talking in poetry without knowing it.

Direction for Q nos 24-26 *Fill in the blanks with the most appropriate prepositions and accordingly select the best option.*

24. _____ what I know _____ Pawan, I hesitate _____ trust him.

    a From, of, to

    b Of, about, in

    c On, of, at

    d For, in, at

25. Cloth should be sold _____ the metre, although many shops sell it _____ the yard.

    a in, in

    b by, of

    c for, by

    d by, by

26. My brother Shyam docs not always agree _________ me.

    a with

    b after

    c to

    d at

Direction for Q nos 27-28 *Fill in the blanks with the correct tense of the verb given in brackets immediately after the blank and accordingly select the best option.*

27. Puneet, the Principal _____ (want) to speak to you.

    a is wanting   **b** wants

    c has been wanting   **d** was wanting

28. Did you think you _____ (see) me somewhere before?

    a was seeing   **b** were seeing

    c have seen   **d** had seen

Direction for Q nos 29–30 *In the passage below, the first and last sentences are identified as A and Z. The remaining four sentences are labelled as P, Q, R and S. Find the correct sequence of these four sentences and select the correct option accordingly.*

29. A Makrana is a small town in Rajasthan.

    P It has been famous for its marble mines since ancient times.

    Q Later on it was used by the British for making the Victoria Memorial in Kolkata.

    R One of these buildings was the Taj Mahal.

    S Four hundred years ago Makrana marble adorned many Mughal buildings.

    Z The same Makrana marble is used today for decorating modern buildings.

    a PQRS   **b** RQPS

    c PSRQ   **d** QRPS

30. A Many people have strong and healthy nails.

    P However, some people have to deal with brittle, dull and lifeless nails.

    Q Pinkish or white nails are an indication of your good health, besides looking pretty.

    R This indicates that the vitamin required for healthy nails is not being taken by them.

    S This vitamin is available in peanuts and leafy green vegetables.

    Z So, eat more peanuts and green vegetables for pretty nails!

    a RPQS   **b** QPSR

    c PQSR   **d** QPRS

Answers

1. c	2. a	3. d	4. c	5. b	6. a	7. d	8. b	9. b	10. d
11. a	12. d	13. c	14. b	15. d	16. d	17. c	18. d	19. d	20. d
21. d	22. a	23. b	24. a	25. d	26. a	27. b	28. d	29. c	30. d

Practice Set 3

Answer & Explanations

① Nouns and Pronouns

Exercise I

1. (c) 2. (c) 3. (a) 4. (c) 5. (b) 6. (b) 7. (a) 8. (b) 9. (b) 10. (c)

Exercise II

1. (b) 2. (c) 3. (a) 4. (c) 5. (b) 6. (c) 7. (c) 8. (a) 9. (b) 10. (b)

Exercise III

1. (a) 2. (b) 3. (a) 4. (a) 5. (b) 6. (c) 7. (c) 8. (b) 9. (a) 10. (b)

Exercise IV

1. (b) 2. (a) 3. (a) 4. (c) 5. (a) 6. (c) 7. (a) 8. (c) 9. (b) 10. (d)

Exercise V

1. (b) 2. (d) 3. (a) 4. (c) 5. (d) 6. (c) 7. (b) 8. (b) 9. (d) 10. (c)

Exercise VI

1. (b) 2. (a) 3. (b) 4. (b) 5. (a) 6. (b) 7. (b) 8. (b) 9. (b) 10. (a)

Exercise VII

1. (d) 2. (b) 3. (a) 4. (c) 5. (b) 6. (c) 7. (a) 8. (b) 9. (c) 10. (d)

② Punctuation and Spelling

Exercise I

1. (c) 2. (a) 3. (b) 4. (d) 5. (a) 6. (b) 7. (b) 8. (c) 9. (d) 10. (a)

Exercise II

1. (b) 2. (d) 3. (a) 4. (c) 5. (b) 6. (c) 7. (d) 8. (a) 9. (c) 10. (b)

Exercise III

1. (c) 2. (b) 3. (d) 4. (d) 5. (c) 6. (b) 7. (c) 8. (b) 9. (a) 10. (a)

Exercise IV

1. (a) 2. (d) 3. (c) 4. (c) 5. (b) 6. (d) 7. (a) 8. (d) 9. (b) 10. (c)

Exercise V

1. (b) 2. (a) 3. (c) 4. (d) 5. (a) 6. (b) 7. (d) 8. (c) 9. (b) 10. (d)

Exercise VI

1. (d) 2. (a) 3. (b) 4. (c) 5. (c) 6. (b) 7. (c) 8. (d) 9. (b) 10. (c)
11. (d) 12. (a)

③ Prepositions

Exercise I

1. (c) 2. (d) 3. (b) 4. (a) 5. (b) 6. (a) 7. (d) 8. (b) 9. (c) 10. (b)

Exercise II

1. (a) 2. (d) 3. (b) 4. (b) 5. (c) 6. (a) 7. (c) 8. (c) 9. (d) 10. (b)

Exercise III

1. (c) 2. (a) 3. (c) 4. (a) 5. (c) 6. (b) 7. (b) 8. (a) 9. (d) 10. (d)

Exercise IV

1. (a)	2. (d)	3. (b)	4. (c)	5. (b)	6. (d)	7. (d)	8. (c)	9. (a)	10. (c)

Exercise V

1. (b)	2. (c)	3. (a)	4. (d)	5. (b)	6. (a)	7. (d)	8. (c)	9. (c)	10. (d)
11. (a)	12. (a)	13. (b)	14. (b)	15. (c)	16. (d)				

④ Determiners

Exercise I

1. (d)	2. (c)	3. (a)	4. (b), (a)	5. (d)	6. (c)	7. (d)	8. (a)	9. (a)	10. (a), (a)
11. (d)	12. (c)	13. (c), (d)	14. (d)	15. (a)	16. (a), (a)	17. (c)	18. (b), (c)	19. (a), (a)	20. (b),(c),(a)

Exercise II

1. (b)	2. (d)	3. (c)	4. (b)	5. (b)	6. (a)	7. (d), (a)	8. (c)	9. (a)	10. (d), (c)

Exercise III

1. (a)	2. (d)	3. (a)	4. (a)	5. (b)	6. (c)	7. (b)	8. (b)	9. (c)	10. (b)

Exercise IV

1. (b)	2. (d)	3. (a)	4. (c)	5. (a)	6. (d)	7. (c)	8. (c)	9. (b)	10. (d)

⑤ Conjunctions

Exercise I

1. (c)	2. (d)	3. (b)	4. (d)	5. (a)	6. (b)	7. (c)	8. (d)	9. (d)	10. (b)

Exercise II

1. (a)	2. (d)	3. (c)	4. (b)	5. (c)	6. (a)	7. (d)	8. (b)	9. (c)	10. (d)

Exercise III

1. (b)	2. (c)	3. (a)	4. (a)	5. (b)	6. (d)/(b)	7. (c)	8. (d)	9. (b)	10. (c)

Exercise IV

1. (d)	2. (d)	3. (c)	4. (d)	5. (b)	6. (a)	7. (b)	8. (a)	9. (c)	10. (b)/(c)

Exercise V

1. (d)	2. (c)	3. (b)	4. (b)	5. (c)	6. (d)	7. (c)	8. (a)	9. (b)	10. (b)

⑥ Modals

Exercise I

1. (a)	2. (c)	3. (b)	4. (d)	5. (d)	6. (a)	7. (d)	8. (c)	9. (c)	10. (c)

Exercise II

1. (c)	2. (a)	3. (c)	4. (a)	5. (d)	6. (b)	7. (d)	8. (a)	9. (b)	10. (a)

Exercise III

1. (c)	2. (c)	3. (b)	4. (d)	5. (a)	6. (d)	7. (c)	8. (b)	9. (d)	10. (a)

Exercise IV

1. (c)	2. (d)	3. (d)	4. (b)	5. (a)	6. (b)	7. (c)	8. (b)	9. (b)	10. (d)
11. (b)	12. (d)	13. (c)	14. (d)	15. (a)					

⑦ Tenses

Exercise I

| 1. (b) | 2. (d) | 3. (b) | 4. (c) | 5. (c) | 6. (d) | 7. (a) | 8. (d) | 9. (c) | 10. (b) |

Exercise II

| 1. (a) | 2. (c) | 3. (d) | 4. (b) | 5. (d) | 6. (a) | 7. (b) | 8. (c) | 9. (d) | 10. (c) |

Exercise III

| 1. (d) | 2. (d) | 3. (b) | 4. (c) | 5. (b) | 6. (d) | 7. (a) | 8. (b) | 9. (d) | 10. (c) |
| 11. (d) | 12. (a) | 13. (c) | 14. (c) | 15. (a) | 16. (b) | 17. (d) | 18. (b) | 19. (b) | 20. (b) |

Exercise IV

| 1. (d) | 2. (c) | 3. (b) | 4. (a) | 5. (b) | 6. (c) | 7. (d) | 8. (b) | 9. (c) | 10. (d) |

⑧ Active and Passive Voice

Exercise I

| 1. (c) | 2. (b) | 3. (a) | 4. (b) | 5. (d) | 6. (c) | 7. (d) | 8. (a) | 9. (b) | 10. (b) |

Exercise II

| 1. (c) | 2. (d) | 3. (b) | 4. (a) | 5. (c) | 6. (b) | 7. (a) | 8. (d) | 9. (d) | 10. (b) |

Exercise III

| 1. (d) | 2. (a) | 3. (c) | 4. (b) | 5. (d) | 6. (c) | 7. (b) | 8. (a) | 9. (c) | 10. (d) |

Exercise IV

| 1. (b) | 2. (a) | 3. (d) | 4. (b) | 5. (c) | 6. (c) | 7. (d) | 8. (a) | 9. (b) | 10. (a) |

⑨ Direct and Indirect Speech

Exercise I

| 1. (d) | 2. (c) | 3. (b) | 4. (d) | 5. (a) | 6. (d) | 7. (b) | 8. (c) | 9. (b) | 10. (c) |

Exercise II

| 1. (b) | 2. (a) | 3. (c) | 4. (b) | 5. (c) | 6. (a) | 7. (d) | 8. (d) | 9. (d) | 10. (c) |

⑩ Sentence Rearrangement

Exercise I

| 1. (d) | 2. (c) | 3. (a) | 4. (b) | 5. (c) | 6. (d) | 7. (b) | 8. (a) | 9. (c) | 10. (d) |

Exercise II

| 1. (c) | 2. (d) | 3. (b) | 4. (a) | 5. (b) | 6. (c) | 7. (d) | 8. (d) | 9. (b) | 10. (a) |

⑪ Synonyms and Antonyms

Exercise I

| 1. (a) | 2. (c) | 3. (d) | 4. (b) | 5. (c) | 6. (d) | 7. (a) | 8. (b) | 9. (c) | 10. (d) |

Exercise II

| 1. (c) | 2. (d) | 3. (b) | 4. (d) | 5. (b) | 6. (c) | 7. (a) | 8. (c) | 9. (d) | 10. (c) |

Exercise III

1. (c)	2. (d)	3. (b)	4. (c)	5. (a)	6. (d)	7. (b)	8. (b)	9. (d)	10. (c)

Exercise IV

1. (c)	2. (d)	3. (b)	4. (a)	5. (c)	6. (d)

Exercise V

1. (b)	2. (d)	3. (c)	4. (b)	5. (a)	6. (a)	7. (c)	8. (d)	9. (d)	10. (c)

12 Idioms and Phrases

Exercise I

1. (d)	2. (a)	3. (c)	4. (d)	5. (c)	6. (b)	7. (d)	8. (b)	9. (a)	10. (c)

Exercise II

1. (b)	2. (d)	3. (a)	4. (c)	5. (b)	6. (c)	7. (d)	8. (a)	9. (b)	10. (c)

Exercise III

1. (c)	2. (d)	3. (a)	4. (b)	5. (d)	6. (c)	7. (b)	8. (c)	9. (a)	10. (d)

Exercise IV

1. (a)	2. (d)	3. (b)	4. (c)	5. (b)	6. (d)	7. (c)	8. (a)	9. (d)	10. (c)

13 Analogy

Exercise I

1. (d) The second results from the first.
2. (c) The second is the action of the first.
3. (a) The second results due to the first.
4. (c) The first is part of the second.
5. (b) The first is used for doing the second.
6. (a) The second is used by the first for motion.
7. (d) The first causes the second.
8. (b) The second is the function of the first.
9. (d) The first is a characteristic of the second.
10. (b) The first is worn on the second.

Exercise II

1. (b) The second operation on the first restores its previous condition.
2. (d) The first is part of the second.
3. (a) The first gives the status of the second.
4. (c) The first measures the second.
5. (d) The first is part of the second.
6. (b) The first is the reverse of the second.
7. (c) The first is stationed in the second.
8. (a) The first is situated inside the second.
9. (a) The second belongs to the first.
10. (b) The first is found on the second.

Exercise III

1. (c) All others are real animals (dragon is a mythical animal).
2. (a) All others are round in shape.
3. (d) All others can usually operate on batteries.
4. (b) All others are for carrying passengers.
5. (c) All others are negative emotions.
6. (d) All others are for residence.
7. (b) All others are countable.
8. (d) All others float on water.
9. (c) All others are part of the basic structure of a house
10. (d) All others are normally worn in winter only.

14 Cloze Test

Exercise I

1. (c)	2. (d)	3. (b)	4. (c)	5. (b)	6. (a)	7. (b)	8. (c)	9. (b)	10. (d)
11. (b)	12. (a)	13. (c)	14. (d)	15. (a)	16. (b)	17. (d)	18. (c)	19. (b)	20. (d)

Exercise II

1. (c)	2. (b)	3. (d)	4. (d)	5. (b)	6. (a)	7. (c)	8. (b)	9. (d)	10. (a)

Exercise III

1. (d)	2. (c)	3. (a)	4. (b)	5. (c)	6. (d)	7. (b)	8. (a)	9. (c)	10. (d)

15 Reading Comprehension

Exercise I

1. (c) Refer to sentence 2 of fourth paragraph.
2. (b) Refer to sentence 2 to of last paragraph.
3. (d) Refer to sentence 2 of the second paragraph.
4. (b)
5. (c) The other three options do not make the sentence meaningful.

Exercise II

1. (d) Refer to the third sentence of the second paragraph.
2. (b) Refer to the second sentence of the last paragraph.
3. (a) This is the dictionary meaning.
4. (c) This option fits best in the sentence.
5. (b) Refer to the third paragraph.

Exercise III

1. (d) This is the only option which can be understood from this sentence, as he could make his own telescope without even seeing the Dutch inventor's spyglass.
2. (d) Refer to the last sentence of the second paragraph.
3. (a) The first two sentences of the last paragraph tell us that this option is not true. All the other options are mentioned at various places in the passage.
4. (b) This is the dictionary meaning.
5. (c) This option fits best in the sentence.

Exercise IV

1. (d)   2. (a)   3. (d)   4. (b)   5. (c)

Exercise V

1. (a) Refer to the first paragraph.
2. (b) Refer to the fourth sentence of the second paragraph.
3. (d) Refer to the second sentence of the fourth paragraph.
4. (c) This is the dictionary meaning.
5. (b) This is the dictionary meaning.

Exercise VI

1. (c) This is a general observation which has been explained throughout the passage. All the other options are part of it.
2. (a) This option has not been mentioned in the passage.
3. (d) The use of the word 'unfortunate' expresses an attitude of sympathy.
4. (b) This is the dictionary meaning.
5. (c) This option fits best in the sentence.

Exercise VII

1. (b) Refer to the first sentence of the first paragraph and the first sentence of the second paragraph.
2. (c) Refer to the last two sentences of the passage.
3. (d) Refer to the first sentence of the passage. All other options are not true as mentioned at various places in the passage.
4. (a) This is the dictionary meaning.
5. (d) This option fits best in the sentence.

Exercise VIII

1. (d)   2. (c)   3. (d)   4. (b)   5. (a)

16 Writing Skills

Exercise I

1. (b)   2. (d)   3. (c)   4. (c)   5. (d)   6. (a)   7. (b)   8. (a)   9. (c)   10. (d)
11. (b)   12. (b)

Exercise II

1. (b)   2. (d)   3. (d)   4. (a)   5. (a)   6. (b)   7. (a)   8. (c)   9. (d)   10. (c)